Women Against Hunger

A SKETCHBOOK JOURNEY

Women Against Hunger

A SKETCHBOOK JOURNEY

Betty LaDuke

Africa World Press, Inc.

P.O. Box 1892
Trenton, NJ 08607

P.O. Box 48
Asmara, ERITREA

Africa World Press, Inc.

P.O. Box 1892   P.O. Box 48

Trenton, NJ 08607   Asmara, ERITREA

Cover Painting by Betty LaDuke
Women's Solidarity: Spirit of Credit With Education

Book Design by Mary Jo Heidrick

Library of Congress Cataloging-in-Publication Data

LaDuke, Betty
    Women against hunger : a sketchbook journey / Betty LaDuke.
        p.   cm.
   ISBN 0-86543-605-3 (cloth). -- ISBN 0-86543-606-1 (pbk.)
   1. Women in development--Case studies. 2. Women in development--Pictorial works. 3. Women in community development--Case studies.
4. Women in community development--Pictorial works. 5. Freedom from Hunger Campaign--Pictorial works. 6. LaDuke, Betty--Notebooks, sketchbooks, etc. 7. LaDuke, Betty--Journeys. I. Title.
HQ1240.L33   1997
305.42--dc21   97-13313
                                                   CIP

Dedicated to

William and

Florence Schneider

for their long-term

commitment to

Freedom from Hunger

and to helping people

help themselves.

Acknowledgments

The opportunity to create this Sketchbook Journey, *Women Against Hunger,* has been an exciting challenge. I want to thank Freedom from Hunger and its President, Christopher Dunford, as well as Vice-President Ellen Vor der Bruegge, and Associate Vice-President Kathleen Sacks for encouraging my visits to their program sites on four continents where I observed women coming together in a process of social change. They believed an artist's perspective would offer a unique view of these Credit With Education programs in action. Throughout this project, Claire Thomas, development director, has been a guiding light.

My visits to Credit With Education programs where I sketched and interacted with the women and their families was facilitated by Frances Bienpo in Ghana, Ayeli Foli in Burkina Faso, Phonglikit Luskonant in Thailand, and Fredie Escalier in Bolivia. Elaine Ricketts introduced me to the Community Health Adviser Network in the United States. The insights I then gained inspired many paintings and etchings created later at the journey's end, in my home studio.

While I enjoy sketching, even when curious villagers crowded around to see how pen and ink lines gradually form a recognizable image, the creating of written impressions is always a more difficult process for me. Therefore, I am especially grateful for Jason Westigard's sensitive editing of the written commentary that accompanies the art and for the creative efforts of Mary Jo Heidrick, graphic designer. Once again, I am pleased to be published by Kassahun Checole, Red Sea Press.

Women Against Hunger
A SKETCHBOOK JOURNEY

BETTY LaDUKE

Contents

CELEBRATING WOMEN'S SOLIDARITY:
Reflections on a Sketchbook Journey

*The growth of a frail flower in a path up
has sometimes shattered and split a rock.
A tough will counts. So does desire. So does
a rich soft wanting. Without rich wanting,
nothing arrives.*

Carl Sandburg
The People Yes

A Freedom from Hunger representative, Johannes Troost, knocked on my Ashland, Oregon studio door in 1992. He came at the suggestion of Bill and Florence Schneider, long-time friends of mine and supporters of this non-profit foundation dedicated since 1946 to eradicating chronic hunger and malnutrition. The Schneiders felt there were some parallels between my drawings, paintings, and prints inspired by my experiences in Africa, Latin America, and Asia and the goal of Freedom from Hunger in those areas of the world.

Johannes, in turn, was intrigued by the life-affirming images in my work that symbolically portrayed women's strength in a context of cultural affirmation. He explained that the Freedom from Hunger program was based on encouraging women's initiative in the self-generation of survival activities, by providing them with short-term loans or credit for their activity expansion. In addition, the women received health education related to nutrition, disease prevention, and family planning through a program known as Credit with Education. Johannes suggested that I consider visiting Freedom from Hunger project sites to sketch and photograph day-to-day village life (Figs. 1 and 2), as well as the specific activities stimulated by the Credit with Education program. My interpretation of program highlights could then offer others a personal view of the individuals who *comprise* the facts and statistics which reflect the successful implementation of this innovative program. These sketches would then be included in a book to celebrate Freedom from Hunger's half century (1946–1996) of dedication to building solidarity among women.

As I had already planned for the following summer an art-research journey to Africa and there was nothing I loved more when traveling than sketching, the proposal interested me. In addition, my sketches would also serve to inspire the mythical paintings and etchings that evolve at the journey's end in my home studio. Meanwhile, I resolved to remain non-committal about the success of Freedom from Hunger's programs until I actually saw them for myself. The word "hunger" was frightening, as it immediately brought to mind media images of massive starvation in Africa and Eastern Europe due to drought and war. I then reminisced about my experiences as a witness of hunger and the use of a sketchbook for self-expression.

1. Market Day, Burkina Faso

I realized that I had never gone hungry, but my father had. I remembered listening to his constant stories about the Ukrainian village of his youth, where cold, hunger, pogroms, and war were persistent facts of life until he emigrated to the United States in 1928. He never forgot his hunger, and both my parents have always been concerned about other people's hunger. As a child growing up in the Bronx during World War II, I remember accompanying my mother up and down tenement stairs to collect donations for the striking coal miners of Pennsylvania or for war refugees.

In the future, food and the lack of food were to become significant themes for my art. While attending the Harlem High School of Music and Art, my sketchbook became a companion with which to explore and record my impressions of New York's diverse ethnic peoples and neighborhoods. I particularly enjoyed markets and the lively interaction between vendors and buyers. *Bagel Lady* and *Garlic Vendor* were early portraits. The sketchbook also accompanied me to college in Denver and

BURKINA FASO

2. On the Farm, Burkina Faso

Cleveland, and then during a venturesome summer experience down the Mississippi River, where I came in touch with deeply-entrenched racism.

The sketchbook and my art continued to be my link to cultural experiences. My world view expanded when I received an art scholarship to the Instituto Allende in San Miguel, Mexico. During this period (1953–1956), I had a unique opportunity to live and work among the Otomi Indians. I was hired by Patrimonio Indigenista del Valle de Mesquital, a Mexican government–United Nations organization established to mainstream the Otomis. They wanted me to paint murals on school patio walls that would symbolically reflect the cultural heritage and future aspirations of the Otomi people. I laugh when remembering that, for payroll purposes, my name was listed as Pedro Bernadino and I was paid the wages of chief brick layer.

For one year, I became an intimate observer of the Otomi life cycle and their dependency on the arid soil where only the thorny mesquite and maguey cactus thrived. Otomi families

VIEWS OF HUNGER SILHOUETTED AGAINST THE CONCRETE OF SKYSCRAPERS OR THE ARID LANDSCAPE. GLAZED EYES, SKELETAL BODIES, A HAND HELD OUT OR AN EMPTY BOWL, BUT WHO TO FILL IT? THE BUSINESS INSPECTOR ON THE BUS TO HARDWAR SPOKE OF KARMA- FATE AND BELIEF IN GOD WHICH HELPS THE HUNGRY TRANSCEND THEIR HUNGER. THE TEACHER FROM BOMBAY LAMENTED THAT KNOWLEDGE WAS NOT REQUIRED BY THOSE WITH HUNGRY BELLIES.

THE INDUSTRIALIST ON THE PLANE TO DELHI INFORMED ME, "EVERYONE'S THRESHOLD FOR PAIN OR HUNGER IS DIFFERENT, A MEAL MISSED BY AN INDIAN IS NOT THE SAME AS DINNER MISSED BY AN AMERICAN."

THE INDIA STUDIES EXPERT FROM THE UNIVERSITY OF MOSCOW USED THE WORD ANANDA, DEFINED AS HAPPINESS. "THEY HAVE ANANDA." "BUT WHAT ABOUT HUNGER"? "NEVER MIND, THEY ARE CHILDLIKE, THEY HAVE ANANDA".

NEEDLESS TO SAY I DID NOT ASK THOSE WITH OUTSTRETCHED HANDS OR THE EMPTY BOWL THEIR VIEW OF THEIR HUNGER.

3. Hunger in India

depended on the sale of their artesania (arts and crafts) at the weekly market to earn the necessary pesos to purchase their staples of corn, beans, and chili. They were resourceful, hardworking people, but powerless and exploited by urban entrepreneurs who paid the Otomis less than a living wage in order to increase their own profits. As a result, the Otomis were frequently hungry.

Eight years later, I joined the faculty of Southern Oregon State College and during my first sabbatical, in 1972, I visited India. Hunger was prevalent in some areas, and I tried to understand the hungry individuals' perspective, as well as that of the onlooker. How should the gnawing, numbing sensation of hunger be interpreted (Fig. 3).

Through the years, with other sabbaticals, grants, and self-financing, I continued my annual sketchbook journeys in Asia as well as Latin America and Africa to research the link between women's art and the process of social change. I continued to witness political power struggles, hunger, and women's resistance, which I recorded in several publications. At the journeys' end, I also painted my impressions of hunger, on large canvases, such as *Los Olvidados* or "The Forgotten Ones" as well as impressions of women's strength and courage, such as " Africa: Birdwomen, Keepers of the Peace" Now I would extend my observations in a new direction: *Women Against Hunger: A Sketchbook Journey.*

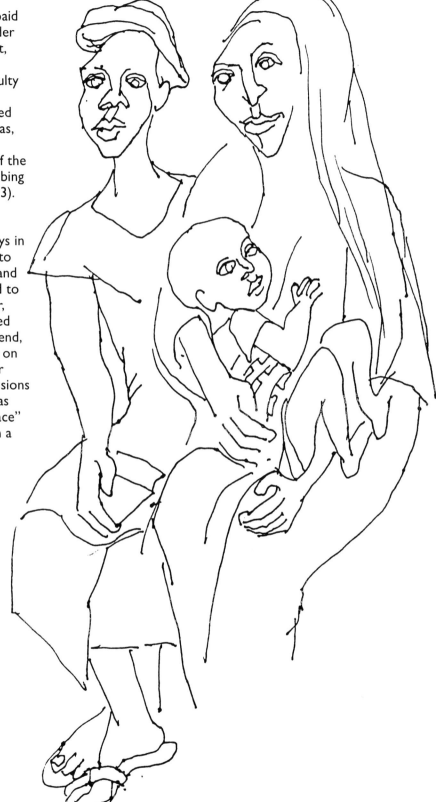

4. *Mothers and children, Burkina Faso*

My travel to Freedom from Hunger project sites began in Africa in 1993 and concluded in the Mississippi Delta region of the United States in 1995. There were physical adjustments from the hot, humid weather of fishing villages and farming communities in Africa, Asia, and the Southern United States, to the high altitude and cool climate of Bolivia. Everywhere, except in the United States, most roads were unpaved and travel was difficult in the dry season and a precarious adventure in the rainy season. While climate as well as foods, customs, and traditions varied, the life cycle—that is, people's dependency on their immediate environment for survival—was very similar (except in the United States) to what I had witnessed among the Otomis 40 years earlier.

I noted how Credit with Education was modified to accommodate different situations. The program was implemented through credit associations and amatrices in Ghana and Burkina Faso, Banco Communales and *promotores* in Bolivia, Credit Associations and field workers in Thailand, and Community Health Advisor Networks (CHANs) and Community Health Advisors (CHAs) in the United States.

I enjoyed meeting with the staff in each location and incorporating their voices and insights. But the most exhilarating aspect of my trip was meeting the women involved in the projects and seeing their determination to make positive change for their families and communities (Fig. 4 and Fig. 5).

I hope others will now vicariously enjoy experiencing this sketchbook journey with me and observe how women grow from "frail flowers" into hearty roses and orchids, as they confront and combat their chronic hunger and malnutrition and turn isolation and despair into hope.

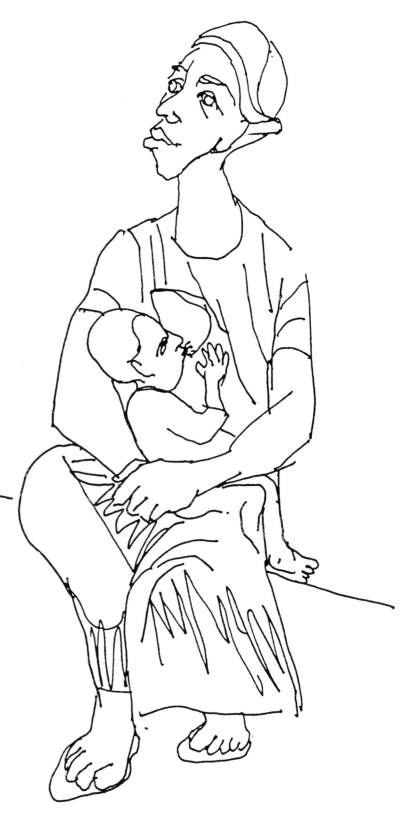

5. Mother and child, Burkina Faso

[1] Betty LaDuke, *Compañeras: Women's Art and Social Change in Latin America* (City Lights, 1985); Betty LaDuke, *Africa Through the Eyes of Women Artists* (Africa World Press, 1991); and Betty LaDuke, *Women Artists, Multicultural Visions* (Red Sea Press, 1992).

2 **AFRICA:** Ghana and Burkina Faso
Credit Associations and Amatrices

1. *Smoking Fish*

Along West Africa's Atlantic coast, from Senegal's Goree Island to Ghana's Cape Castle, one can step from scorching sunlight into the damp darkness of stone-walled rooms still filled with the echoes of slave cargo three centuries past. However, during my first Freedom from Hunger journey, rather than focusing on the past, I would focus on the future, visiting credit associations extending from the coastal fishing villages of Ghana to the farm-dominated country of Burkina Faso. It would be an intense three-week trip. In the process of documenting women's economic projects and observing their day-to-day activities (Fig. I), I would become aware of the incredible resourcefulness, camaraderie, and pride generated by the credit associations.

GHANA
My first contact in Ghana was Freedom from Hunger director Francis Bienpo, a soft-spoken man in his mid-50s who met me at the Accra airport. Over dinner that evening, Francis told me he had previously made much more money working for the International Monetary Fund and as a Ghana bank administrator, but he was happier now working for Freedom from Hunger. The job kept him very busy, and although he and his staff had a small office in Accra, the capital, most often they were traveling by jeep transport to visit the growing number of credit associations located in this region of Ghana.

Since it was my first program visit, I was concerned about what I would see the following day when we traveled to several credit association meetings. I wanted to know what to expect, as the word "hunger" brought to my mind numerous media images of mass starvation and intense suffering. Francis immediately clarified that Freedom from Hunger's strategy was aimed at the economically poor, but not at the unproductive, the incapacitated, or the disabled. The program goal was to honor poor but capable women, who were already engaged in income-generating activities (Fig. 2). According to Francis, it was *important* to offer these women a push, an impetus to improve or expand upon their activities through the securing of bank loans. Individually, they would not normally qualify for such loans, but once organized collectively, they found the banks willing to work with them.

Although the loans were a big part of the program, Francis made it clear that the educational aspect of the program was equally important. The women were taught about nutrition, disease prevention, and family planning.

According to Francis, although the credit associations varied in membership from 28 to 40 women, the routines were similar. Each had elected officers and an amatrice, or group facilitator to oversee the financial transactions and provide the educational component. (Fig. 3). The amatrices were young men or women with a high school or college education who lived at or near a project site. They met with five to fifteen credit associations per week and also reached out to form new groups. Francis explained that communication was difficult because most roads were unpaved, and just reaching some of the hillside villages with the motorbikes the amatrices were allotted for travel was precarious during dry season and a miracle during the rainy season.

Aboadze and Abouzi

The next morning, within two hours of leaving the crowds, the traffic, and the modern high-rise buildings of Accra, we arrived at the village of Aboadze. Although the surrounding coastal region was well-visited by tourists of the infamous colonial slave-holding castles at Elmira, Cape Coast, and Dixie Cove, Aboadze seemed almost completely bypassed, not only by tourists but by Western necessities such as electricity and roads. There were, however, many churches of varied denominations and one pharmacy.

As I looked around, I was surprised by the number of people that emerged from the jumble of pastel-painted wood-and-stucco homes interlaced with mud-and-brick smoking and drying ovens. The villages seemed alive with activity. Mothers attended to babies while hovering over large basins of fish. Young children played. Goats and chickens scampered about (Figs. 4 and 5). It was immediately obvious that village life was dominated by fishing and fish processing. Because the cycle of fishing was new for me, I was happy to be invited to stay for several days, to participate and sketch the daily rhythms of life. Soon I would come to think of village life as a competitive mating dance between men and women, ocean and land.

Christiana Atta Peters (Fig. 6), the local pharmacist and only Aboadze resident who spoke English fluently, was my guide during my three-day visit. Educated as a pharmacist in Germany, she now sold some medicines from the small pharmacy that occupied one room of her small home. She was well known, as she assisted during childbirth, dispensed malaria pills, and took care of many medical emergencies.

That day, walking (as we would for the next three days) the two kilometers along the shore between Aboadze and the neighboring village of Abouzi, Christiana and I were greeted by fishermen mending their nets or sitting in groups playing checkers on makeshift

2. Three Generations of Abuesi Fish Processors

3. Financial Records and Transactions

boards with bottlecap pieces. Christiana explained that the daily routine was much different for men than for women. Most days men would fish, leaving before sunrise and returning in the early afternoon, but when the ocean was stormy and the fishermen determined it was too risky to take out their small, wooden vessels fitted with outboard motors, they could "ease around," drink, and play games. For the women, survival activities were much more constant, like the ceaseless internal breathing of the ocean. Not only did the women spend most of their days smoking and drying fish as they prepared to take it to the market, but during lulls in the fish-processing the women kept busy tending to children, preparing food for the family, or developing other business activities.

It was fascinating to realize how men and women were mutually dependent but also competitive (Fig. 7). The men depend on the women because there is no cold storage or canning facility and the fish must be immediately smoked and dried or it will spoil. The women, of course, depend on the men to catch the fish. The men sold the women the fish at the highest possible price, but with credit association loans, the women could now negotiate in their own favor because they could pay for the fish immediately instead of having to pay the fishermen an exorbitant sum after it was processed and sold.

As there were no hotels in Aboadze, I was fortunate to be invited to eat and sleep at the home of Christiana's friend Janet. She was a warm, friendly person but because she didn't speak English and I didn't know the local dialect, it was obviously difficult to talk to her. However, we both did a lot of smiling and hand gestures, and after I showed her the wallet pictures of my children and grandchildren, I felt we shared a common bond. Her children were also grown, and her two grandchildren stayed with her during their summer-school vacation, to help her with the daily activities while their mother worked.

The days were very busy for Janet. In the morning she would prepare a spicy fish sauce for the midday meal, and in the afternoon she would make flour chips. These chips were her primary means of self-support, and during my stay I had ample opportunity to observe her unceasing involvement in producing, packaging, and selling these chips. The production took place in her yard, where she had a table and rolled out long pieces of flour dough. She then fed the dough into a pasta machine and as she turned the

4. Goats and Chickens Scamper About

5. Village Life

6. Christiana atta Peters, local pharmacist

handle the dough was cut into long, thin strips which were then cut with scissors into two-inch lengths. Meanwhile, a pan filled with oil was heated over a low stove, and Janet deep-fried her chips until they were crisp and golden-brown. She then piled them high onto several large aluminum basins. Over several days, in the shade of her patio, she methodically filled hundreds of little plastic bags with her chips and a few carefully counted peanuts. Sometimes her grandchildren or a neighbor helped with this endless task. I even tried briefly, but preferred instead to draw (Fig. 8).

With her Freedom from Hunger loan just a month before, Janet was able to buy the pasta-cutting machine that now saved her hours of production time and allowed her to increase her volume. Now, she had no trouble selling her chips and she even hired several young girls to carry the chips to sell to the fishermen when the boats came in. I began to realize Janet and her chips were very popular as throughout the day people stopped by the house to buy chips and chat while Janet kept working.

Association Meeting

During my second day at the village, Francis returned to inquire about my well-being and accompany me to my first credit association meeting. When we arrived at the church where it was to take place, many of the village women had already assembled and soon after, John Assouan, the young amatrice, arrived on his motorbike. John briefly introduced me as a Freedom from Hunger representative with a sketchbook, and then the meeting began (Fig. 9). As I sat on a bench beside Francis so that he could translate for me, I was surprised by the formality of the meeting. It began with a prayer and roll call by the secretary. Late arrivals had to pay a small fine to the treasurer. (Francis later told me that if a woman was absent more than twice during the 16-week loan-repayment cycle, she would be disqualified from future participation, as tardiness was a significant problem.) Next, the secretary methodically collected the loan payments and carefully recorded the transactions in a large ledger. Finally, after everything was checked, the president announced to the group that all payments had been made, and the education portion of the meeting could begin.

7. Men Fishing

8. Janet atta Peters and Her Flour Chips

As John began to instruct the women about health issues, it was interesting to observe how he asked the women questions such as, "If I know I can vaccinate my child against six childhood diseases, why will I not send my child for a vaccination on time?" The women were not shy and several raised their hands to respond, offering excuses that evoked laughter. One woman even stood and waved her arms before the group as she energetically enacted an anecdote about the evils of procrastination (Fig, 10).

After the meeting I was introduced to Hannah Sankah, the president of Aboadze's credit association, who invited me to visit her home so I could see her business enterprise. After walking through a maze of narrow lanes we arrived at the open, bright-blue painted door of Hannah's house. Beside the door was a small table with two large clay pots filled with a traditional sweetened corn beverage that Hannah told us she produced in addition to tarts (Fig. 11). She welcomed us and then proceeded to demonstrate how she made her tarts. She rolled out her sweet flour dough and then cut and folded each triangular section into a little pyramid shape which she placed on a cookie sheet for baking.

9. *Aboadze Credit Association Members*

I soon learned that Hannah's husband had died 18 years earlier and she had raised five children alone. Hannah was very proud that she managed to support her children so they could all attend school and have professions such as refrigerator mechanic, tailor, seamstress, bookkeeper, and accountant. Hannah's business was very successful; every other day she baked tarts and had no trouble selling them all. Her future goal was to bake bread, which required a larger outlay of cash and access to ovens. She was excited about the prospect of expanding her business and realized it was a good possibility. In the future, after her smaller loans were paid back, the principal on subsequent loans would gradually be increased.

Day-to-Day Life

One of my favorite activities during my three-day stay was to walk the two kilometers between Aboadze and Abouzi and sketch credit association members at their various activities. There were many simple, thatched shelters where women fried doughnuts, beignets, or millet cakes and sold roasted corn (Fig. 12). In addition to sketching, I enjoyed tasting all these treats, and appreciated the hospitality that was extended to me, especially when the women were told by Christiana that I was a Freedom from Hunger representative. Each day there was always so much to see and sketch (Fig. 13). One day we saw a woman who could be described as a walking store; she carried a tray on her head filled with an assortment of cosmetics, perfumes, soaps, spices and instant, powdered foods to entice prospective buyers.

On stormy days when we walked close to the ocean, it was delightful to look at fishermen's boats resting on the shore (Fig. 14). I observed their decorative details and interesting names such as *Feed Yourself, God Never Sleeps, If You Have God No Fears, Sea Never Dry,* and (a bit to my surprise) *Rambo.* Christiana explained that there were special houses where the fishermen lived during the bumper season, so when it was time to fish it was easier to awaken the crew. Fishing was a precarious job because boats often capsized, so every morning church bells rang through the village beckoning the residents to pray for the fishermen.

The Fishermen Return

On the last day of my visit, the ocean calmed and the men went out to fish. Late that afternoon, I was able to see the boats return and watch the village come alive with excitement. Children attending the school at the top of the hill were the first to see the fishermen return. When they recognized the boats' brightly colored flags from the windows of their schoolhouse, they ran to meet the boats and welcome home their fathers and other relatives.

Before the boats were hauled to shore by the fishermen, young girls walked waste-deep into the water with aluminum basins on their heads to collect the fish. After the fish were carefully counted out and given to them, the girls rushed with their heavy basins through the village to their particular team of three or more women who were waiting for them by the ovens to begin the fish-drying process (Fig. 15).

I spent many hours that afternoon watching the women work, noticing how they never seemed to waste a movement.

DUNKWA

10. Explaining the Evils of Procrastination

*11. Hanna Sankah Selling Her Tarts
and Corn Beverage*

12. *Making Beignets or Millet Cakes*

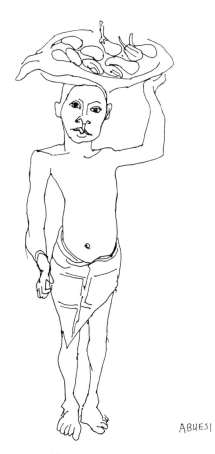

13. Selling Vegetables

ABUESI

14. Fisherman with His Granddaughter
in the Boat

ABOADZE

First they would lay the fish out on framed wire screens. The rectangular screens were then stacked in groups of six and placed in the oven, which was covered with a woven palm lid or a sheet of corrugated metal. The oven was continually fueled with wood for two or three hours, and the screens were periodically rotated. This process was physically exhausting, as the women were constantly on their feet (Fig. 16). The smoked fish were then removed and put into tall, circular drying ovens where they were layered upon a single bamboo shelf for 24 hours. It was interesting to observe how the women worked together in well-coordinated teams, never pausing even to wipe their sweat away until the ovens were loaded. Many women even carried babies on their backs.

Later, I was amazed when Christiana told me fish processing could last as long as four months, from June to September, when teams of women frequently worked around the clock to smoke and dry the fish. During this period, smoke constantly billowed over the village, darkening the days, burning people's eyes and choking them. When the drying process was complete, the fish were packed into large, sturdy baskets for transport by other women to market centers. During the bumper season when fish were plentiful, the women received less money at market than when the fish were more scarce. However, since they had no provisions for storing the oven-dried fish until conditions were more favorable, they sold their processed fish for whatever they could get.

Conclusion

That evening, after returning to Accra by bus, I shared some of my impressions of the Abouzi and Aboadze experience with Francis. Even though language communication had been limited, I had felt welcomed and I was glad that my sketchpad had served as a visual bridge and even a form of village entertainment (Fig. 17). I left the villages with a sense of optimism and a better understanding of how Credit with Education functioned. I now realized what Francis meant by "honoring poor but capable women." The women had extraordinary skills and were resourceful, but needed an extra push to expand and grow, to improve their future as well as that of their children.

BURKINA FASO

After a tedious, 26-hour bus ride, I was relieved to finally arrive in Ouagadougou, the capital of Burkina Faso; however, it was Sunday and I was soon disappointed as the town center seemed to be at rest, with shop doors closed and streets deserted. Reluctantly, I went by taxi to my prearranged hotel room at the edge of town to rest and wait for my scheduled evening appointment with Ayeli Foli, Freedom from Hungers' Burkina Faso coordinator.

That night when we met, I was immediately impressed by Ayeli's warm smile, outgoing exuberance, and bright, patterned dress. I was also grateful she spoke fluent English. Although she thought I would enjoy eating pizza in an air-conditioned restaurant, I told her I would rather eat in a more traditional style, and soon we were enjoying chicken and rice in an outdoor restaurant, which we shared with the mosquitoes.

16. Resting

15. Smoking and Drying Fish

17. *Spirits Rising*

18. Let's Do It

BURKINA FASO
KIENFANGUE

During dinner, I learned Ayeli had been born in West Africa and had grown up in a large family in a village in the nation of Togo. Excelling in school, she had taken the opportunity to study in Switzerland and then come to the United States where she earned her master's degree in public health at Johns Hopkins University.

During my stay in Burkina Faso, Ayeli would be an invaluable guide, sensitizing me to the Freedom from Hunger program and its effect upon women and their families (Fig. 18). Ayeli succinctly summed up Freedom from Hunger's philosophy: "I believe strongly, if you are poor, you are not stupid. You are clever. You are smart. Let's do it."

Ziniare

The next day, as I traveled to the nearby village of Ziniare with Ayeli, and Tico Sanfo, the Freedom From Hunger chauffeur who would also serve as our translator, I sketched the men and women who worked in the millet fields along the road (Fig. 19). With arched backs and hoes in their hands, they relentlessly chopped the weeds away from their millet seedlings (Fig.20). As we drove, Ayeli explained to me that Ziniare was being considered as a future Freedom from Hunger site. The region had been identified in World Bank studies as one with

19. Chopping Weeds

20. Chopping Weeds

21. Dimi Matae with Children and Grandchildren

22. Returning from Pasture

chronic malnutrition and seasonal hunger. Ayeli told me that when we got to the village we would meet with the village Chief, as it was customary to talk with village officials before establishing a link with the women.

After arriving in Ziniare, a small village consisting of clusters of bamboo-and-thatch huts that smoothly blended with the earth, we traveled down a small path primarily traveled by villagers and their donkeys, to the home of Dimi Matae, the village chief. Although it was late afternoon, Dimi, a lean, muscular man with a kind face and a short, white beard, was still hoeing weeds while two of his children were guiding a donkey that pulled a plow. Sanfo translated Mossi, the local language, into French and Ayeli translated the French into English so I was able to learn some basic facts about Dimi.

Dimi, approximately 75, was still hearty and a hard worker. This was surprising, since the average life expectancy in the region was forty-eight years. He came from a long line of village chiefs, a position he inherited when he was about 30 years old. I was beginning to learn that asking people about their age was troublesome, as most did not know the exact date or year of their birth and identity cards were not accurate. Dimi had five wives and calculated 25 children (some were babies) and 35 grandchildren (Fig. 21). Several sons had attended school and one had achieved a high position as an accountant in Ouagadougou. This son when he visited gave Dimi cash gifts, which were much appreciated, especially before the harvest season. Assisted by his children and wives, Dimi worked each day on his four hectares of land, cultivating millet, beans, and corn. But because his family was so large, they could not produce enough and Dimi sold some of his goats between harvest periods to buy food.

When Dimi was asked about village problems, he raised his hands agitatedly and cited lack of access to water. He told us there were only four water pumps to provide for over 100 households or compounds; therefore, it could take women up to three hours a day to wait their turn to pump and haul water.

After we talked for a while, I was glad when Dimi invited us back to his home. His compound was fenced with bamboo and contained many thatched huts—one for each of his wives and her children. As we walked through the compound, I was surprised by all of the activity. Dimi's sons were returning from pasture with goats and sheep (Fig. 22). Women busily pounded millet for the evening meal (Fig. 23). (Throughout Africa, the pounding of millet by women is the counterpart of U.S. women pushing supermarket shopping carts.) The rhythmic pounding of the millet was like a drumbeat calling the men home from the field and providing the pulse beat of life's continuity, the assurance of food.

As we stood in front of Dimi's large rectangular hut, many of his children appeared, and he held the smallest one on his hip while he talked to us. It was nice to see the pride and love he had for his family. However, as I looked around it was evident that his family members' lives weren't easy. The older wives looked worn and tired with breasts hanging low and empty. Most children had spindly legs and swollen bellies—signs of worms or other stomach disorders.

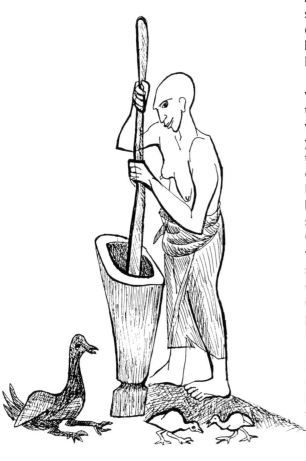

23. Pounding Millet

24. Women Coming Together

Ayeli explained to Dimi that not only could Freedom from Hunger help the women to augment their small business projects such as selling millet cakes on market day, but it could also help educate the women about disease prevention, caring for the children, and family planning. Dimi seemed very responsive and was eager to do whatever was necessary to improve life in the village. Dimi promised he would talk to the women, so that when Ayeli visited again they could establish a firm meeting date to learn more about the credit association.

As we headed back that evening, I couldn't stop thinking about how privileged we seemed to Dimi and his wives. Our hands were not calloused—Ayeli and I held pens rather than hoes—and our clothes were not tattered and faded from too much sun. Dimi and his family were bound to the rhythm of land cultivation and were often at the mercy of the unpredictable weather. Should the rains delay or not come, the consequences would be frightening. City dwellers could not survive without their labor, yet there seemed so little respect for the survival and well-being of the rural farmer.

25. Lucy Sakonde

Kienfangue

    The sun's rays were already intensely hot the next day at 10 a.m. when we arrived at Kienfangue. A credit association meeting was underway, and women, some with babies, gathered under the shade of an expansive banyan tree, making their payments and talking to the amatrice (Fig. 24). Ayeli told me she was impressed with this group's solidarity, as last week all the women had contributed money for one woman who couldn't pay, and today the woman was paying them all back.

    After all the women made their payments, their attention was focused upon three amatrices, who used dolls in their lesson plan on infant diarrhea treatment. The dolls were cheerfully dressed with pants or a skirt and blouse, and the amatrices pretended to give the dolls, supposedly sick with diarrhea, nourishing food. Then they pretended to change and clean the dolls, stressing how they washed their hands with soap to avoid spreading germs and sickness. The amatrices' basic message for surviving this ailment was the need to feed the child extra food

26. Women on the Move

and liquids. The women were also taught about simple sugar and salt solutions for oral rehydration. The women seemed to listen intently and enjoyed the use of the dolls. Ayeli told me these lessons were very important, as diarrhea was the number-one cause of infant death in Africa.

At the conclusion, the amatrices asked the women questions about the presentation they had just seen. The women responded in unison, almost chant-like, with phrases such as, "You must encourage your children to eat and drink, even when they are sick." I was surprised how short the meeting was, but Ayeli explained to me that during the growing season the lesson plan had to be short and simple because the women were impatient to return to the farm. "If they don't work now they won't have food to eat later," Ayeli said.

After the meeting, Lucy Sakonde (Fig. 25), one of the credit association members, invited us to her home to look at her weavings. She rode her bike while we followed her in our car the two kilometers to her home. Old bicycles are a sign of affluence, and it was fun to watch her maneuver around pot holes and wave to neighbors as she rode. When we arrived at her compound, I realized that the economic level of her family was better than most. While most homes were made of bamboo and thatch, her home was made of several large stucco structures with corrugated metal roofs. Her husband's Assembly of God church sat across the road from her home.

Outside of her compound was a large metal loom that had been placed in the shade of a tree. As we gathered around it, Lucy sat at the loom and demonstrated the weaving process. She then proudly showed us some samples of her work. As Ayeli translated, I discovered that Lucy had learned to weave from a neighbor and now had nine years of experience. However, thread was expensive and she seldom created weavings for her own pleasure. Her loom had been made for her in Ouagadougou and was wide enough to produce strips of cloth approximately 20 inches wide by 12 feet long. Four identical strips were necessary to make a complete outfit that consisted of an underskirt, overskirt, and blouse. It took her five days of steady weaving to produce one strip of cloth, but it was difficult to find the time because she also had to care for five children from three to seven years of age.

27. Fermented Bean Cakes

In many ways Lucy's success as a weaver depended upon the success of the crops. She said that during a good harvest year people wanted to look and dress their best for the harvest celebrations and she would get many commissions. However, in the last few years selling hand-loomed cloth had become more difficult with the influx of less-expensive, manufactured cloth from Holland and England. (Throughout Africa there is a brisk business in used clothing from the United States and Europe.) With her credit association loan, Lucy divided her funds into two parts. With one part, she bought cotton thread for weaving cloth. The other she used to purchase ingredients such as oil and salt for the production of beignets, or fried bean cakes, that she sold at the market.

That afternoon when we left Lucy's, I was pleased when Ayeli informed me that today was market day and I would get to see the location where Lucy and others sold their goods. The market took place near the main road under a large grove of trees, and as we walked through the market, I was fascinated by the constant kaleidoscopic movement of people, animals and produce. I began to sketch while Ayeli visited with various credit association members who were buying or selling produce (Fig. 26). I continued to move about, sketching a variety of vendors with their calabashes of yogurt, piles of fruit and fermented bean cakes. The variety of colors, patterns, and textures was startling (Fig. 27).

Sabou, Women Farmers

The next day, during the three-hour car ride from Ouagadougou to Sabou, women were visible working in teams or individually in the millet fields. Their backs were rounded as they stooped over the young green millet plants, chopping weeds with short-handled hoes. I enjoyed drawing them; their arched backs echoed the shape of the round, mud huts clustered behind them (Fig. 28).

Sabou was more developed than the other villages I had seen, and had many shops and vendors with fruit and soda pop. When I arrived at the credit association meeting, I was introduced to the 15 women of the group, who I soon learned were primarily professional farmers (Fig. 29 & 30). During farming season they begin with the first rays of light to farm their own garden plots, and then they farmed for their husbands, before hiring themselves out to work for teachers, local officials or other upper-class people. During the dry season, some women utilized their earnings to make beignets or brew millet beer. It was common for the woman to consume a calabash of beer before going to farm, as it provided quick energy and was nutritious.

Later Ayeli introduced Celicite Quedraogo, who was one of the group amatrices as well as the local, small-branch bank manager. She explained to me that the women wanted to borrow money to expand their farming activities, but before they could borrow the money from Freedom from Hunger, they had to save money to secure the loan. Celicite said it would take the group at least six months. Meanwhile, they were building a sense of group solidarity, receiving some health education and learning how to keep records of financial transactions. When I wondered how the husbands were responding to the women's initiative, she responded, "They are happy, as they know in the future everyone will eat better."

28. Arched Backs

29. Sabou Credit Association Meeting

SABOU

30. Sabou Credit Association Members

Celicite described her role as that of an "advocate, to organize, sensitize and raise the group's awareness about the bank and the possibilities open to them through savings." For many women this was the first time they had ever been able to save money, and saving was very important as it meant food security for the future in times of drought or a family emergency. Celicite was very enthusiastic about her work and very patient with the women; most were illiterate and keeping records was not easy for them.

That evening we slept in a small Sabou hotel that was stifling hot because of the metal roof. Very early the next morning I again walked around with my sketchpad (Fig. 31). The sun was just coming up, so I was surprised to see many very young children already at work. I noticed a young boy—no older than seven or eight–was carrying a heavy log across his shoulders as he walked down the road (Fig. 32). Then, as I sketched one woman working in her garden,

32. Carrying Firewood

SABOU

31. Sabou Sunrise

SABOU

her young granddaughter, barely reaching the height of her elbow, came out carrying a hoe and began to work beside her (Fig. 33). Over breakfast, I told Ayeli what I had seen and she explained that by age five or six, children begin to assist with farming. They were trained by the women, and by age seven they would be ready to help their fathers (Fig. 34). Ayeli assured me that children went to school, but since this was the rainy season, it was also their school vacation.

Conclusion

That afternoon as we left Sabou, I realized that my first Freedom from Hunger journey was coming to an end and I would soon be traveling home to the green, pear-growing valleys of Oregon. I felt inspired and excited by all that I had seen. Although I had visited Africa on six prior occasions to interview women artists, I felt, for the first time, I had gained an intimate understanding of village life. From Ghana's coastal fishing villages to Burkina Faso's millet-producing farms, I was impressed by people's industriousness and their ability to use their limited resources. In my studio, I painted *Women Coming Together, The Spirit of Credit with Education*. In the painting, many women are seated under a tree as they participate in a Credit Association meeting. The tree's form is a woman with branch-like arms reaching up, symbolizing women's solidarity. This vision and others, such as women pounding millet or buying and selling produce at the marketplace, would linger in my mind, reminding me that Africa was a place where there was much sorrow as well as laughter and hope.

But what would stay with me more than anything else were the words of Ayeli. "If you are poor, you are not stupid. You are clever, you are smart. Let's do it!" These words would become a life-affirming chant that would be repeated throughout my Freedom from Hunger journeys.

32. Grandmother Farming

3 **LATIN AMERICA:** Bolivia
Banco Communales and Promotores

In January 1994 I began my second Freedom from Hunger journey, in which I would visit Bolivia. I looked forward to this visit, as I had welcome memories of Bolivia's indigenous culture, centered on Pachamama or Mother Earth, experienced 10 years earlier while researching my book *Compañeras: Women, Art and Social Change in Latin America.* For most Bolivians, Pachamama is the root of their identity. She is a living, spiritual being with whom it is important to maintain a harmonious relationship. Pachamama was venerated at all times, but especially during periods of transition or personal rites of passage. In many ways, the Bolivian veneration of Pachamama reminded me of Mexico's Otomi Indians with whom I had lived and worked almost 40 years earlier. Most indigenous people maintain respect for the earth and the environment, but in Bolivia I would find some contradictions. While Pachamama was respected, women frequently were not.

I arrived in Cochabamba, Bolivia at 9 a.m., as the sun was beginning to warm the surrounding green valleys. En route from the airport to my hotel, the taxi passed through the center of town, and I was able to see the Cochabamba market and plaza, which I remembered from my last visit (Figs. 1–3). The plaza consisted of shops, restaurants, and a gracious cathedral, surrounded by a park where people sought relief from the heat of the day and listened to local bands play every Sunday evening.

With a population of over 100,000, Cochabamba is Bolivia's second largest city. Its cultural amenities and entertainment vary from universities, theaters, and libraries to discos, gourmet restaurants, and cafes serving American hamburgers. However, there is a sharp division between those who have the opportunity to absorb these cultural amenities and those who live on the fringe, counting their coins from one meal to the next. On the hillsides surrounding the town center, the elegant, pastel-painted stucco homes are absent. Clusters of huts, haphazardly constructed with scraps of wood and covered with sheets of corrugated metal, house the rural poor who have come to town in search of work, especially during times of crop failure.

It was before noon when I arrived at the headquarters of Freedom from Hunger. The staff was located in a small house in a residential neighborhood. After meeting Fredie Escalier, the national program director, I was introduced to Jorge Delgado, the regional coordinator, who would be my guide for the first few days of travel. Jorge had prepared an extensive schedule of banco communales for me to attend. We would begin with the nearby villages of Tarata and Cliza, and then travel farther to the remote village of Anzaldo. Although I was tired from my journey, I soon felt revitalized after drinking two cups of mato de coca tea, which minimizes the effect of soroche (altitude sickness). Cochabamba's elevation is over 6000 feet, and I would soon travel to locations as high as 14,000 feet.

1. *Cochabamba Market*

TARATA AND CLIZA

As we passed through the paved streets of Cochabamba and headed down the dusty, unpaved roads to the villages, Jorge, who was soft spoken and seemed shy at first, gradually told me about the area. According to Jorge, people's economic survival was based on farming supplemented by women's artesania or traditional craft production. Most families owned five or fewer hectares of land (one hectare equals 2.47 acres), where they planted corn, potatoes, vegetables, fruit, and peanuts (Fig. 4). They also had some animals (Fig. 5) but ate meat only on special occasions. The needed rains were not always forthcoming, and during the years of drought there was much suffering. Since 1989, when Freedom from Hunger began its programs in the area, 25 banco communales had been established in this region, and seven more were in the process of being inaugurated. Jorge was happy that the demand for communales was great, but disheartened that the growth was slow because of the limited amount of promoters and financial partnerships that could be established.

After driving several kilometers past the old colonial town of Tarata, we arrived in Cliza, a small village of crumbling mud-and-adobe homes. We were a few minutes late, and the women of the banco communal were already assembled at a home waiting for the meeting to begin (Fig. 6). Some sat on a courtyard bench beside an elaborate, enclosed altar containing the Virgin de Carmen. Others sat in the main meeting room on benches or the floor waiting to make their payments. I was intrigued by their patient expressions, and I began to sketch them (Figs. 7 and 8). Most women wore straw hats, and the younger women wore knee-length, multiple-layered skirts which gave them a bell-like appearance. Several women also had children nestled on their backs. The children were secured in brightly-striped carrying blankets which seemed a natural extension of the women's bodies (Fig. 9). Many women had also arrived with spindles or knitting needles in their hands (Figs. 10 and 11). Although they worked throughout the meeting, it was obvious that the bright and intricately patterned clothes they were knitting were for others to wear, as these women wore less expensive, factory-made sweaters made of acrylic yarn.

The meeting began with the usual greetings, announcements, and credit loan payments. After the financial transactions were completed, I enjoyed watching the group's

2. Cochabamba Market

3. Street Vendor

4. Chopping Weeds

education process and observed how the promoters utilized illustrated posters in their teaching. Most of the posters dealt with health topics such as the treatment of infant diarrhea or breast feeding, but some dealt with interpersonal relationships. These seemed to strike a chord with the women. One showed a woman carrying a huge bundle of firewood while her husband walked ahead of her carrying nothing. Another pictured a husband displeased and beating his wife. There was a unanimous murmur of acknowledgment and laughter, as the women recognized their own familiarity with this situation. After putting away the first group of posters, the promoters showed the women pictures demonstrating how men and women could interact as equals. One portrayed a mother dressing young children while the father took older ones to school. Another showed a man doing household chores. The women excitedly discussed these images, surprised that men could be supportive and cooperative.

After the meeting ended, we gave a ride home to several of the promoters. One of them, Yolanda, a short woman with dark sparkling eyes who had worked on the Freedom from Hunger staff for over eight years, gave me some interesting insights about the day-to-day life of a promoter.

According to Yolanda, the promoters worked in pairs and, due to lack of adequate transportation, during the week they frequently slept in the local Tarata office (a room rented

5. Shearing a Sheep

from a family). For most of their travel they used motorbikes, and when their motorbikes were in need of repair they had to walk the eight kilometers from Tarata to Cliza in order to supervise the groups. Yolanda, who was trained as a public health nurse and worked in community health programs in La Paz before coming to Cochabamba, said that the work was challenging, as it took time for the women to trust an outsider.

"At first," said Yolanda, "the doors are closed and it takes a long time until women open themselves and their homes to you and invite you in. But we are good listeners and, gradually, the women do confide many of their personal problems."

One thing Yolanda said she had learned was to never refuse food because it offended people. Yolanda told us a story. Once, after a Banco Communal meeting, she had been stuck without transportation in a village far from Tarata. A member invited her to eat at her house, but when she got there she noticed everything seemed dirty: the plate, the spoon, even the food.

"I didn't want to refuse the food, because I knew it would offend her, so I ate very fast to force myself to eat," said Yolanda. "Unfortunately, the woman thought I liked it and asked me if I wanted more."

Yolanda's dedication was evident, as she continued, "Promoters must plan for the future. We are always thinking

MOSOC RANCHO

GLIZA

6. Women Assembling

about developing new posters, drawings, and methods to educate the women."

When I asked Yolanda about the posters I had seen at the meeting dealing with machismo and the interpersonal relationships of men and women, she emphasized the importance of helping the women realize that machismo or domestic violence is not justifiable behavior.

"If we don't speak up, we will continue to suffer and our sons and husbands will never learn," said Yolanda.

Tarata and the Doll Maker

The next morning we returned to the villages, and this time I got more of a chance to see Tarata, an old colonial town with stone streets, a plaza, and a church. We met up with Yolanda and the other promoters and, as we walked around Tarata, I noticed several women sitting outside their houses, knitting (Figs. 12 and 13). Yolanda told me the women specialized in producing many different things including sweaters, hats, and *ch'uspas* (purses in the form of dolls), designed for the tourist market. Yolanda told me the men traditionally carried their coca leaves in these *ch'uspas* while they farmed or worked in the tin

7. *Laura Rocha Cordova*

mines. According to Yolanda, chewing coca provided relief from the cold, dulled hunger, and enabled people to endure long hours of toil. Coca also provided a temporary sense of well-being and was a basic component of all rituals honoring Pachamama. I was delighted when Yolanda told me that one of Tarata's most widely known doll makers, a banco communal member, lived nearby.

Accompanied by Jorge, and Yolanda, I proceeded to the doll maker's house. After Yolanda knocked on her door, the doll maker, Carmen Blanco, appeared a bit surprised at the crowd that had come to see her dolls. However, she welcomed us all into a long, narrow room containing a dining table and chairs and invited us to be comfortable as she brought a tall cardboard box filled with many completed *ch'uspas*. I knew I would have to buy some to take back as gifts, but I had a problem: They were all so beautiful, I couldn't decide which ones. Each knitted doll seemed to have its own personality that emanated from the embroidered facial expressions and a selection of saturated colors that were juxtaposed in intricate patterns. The doll heads and limbs were made of an undyed, white wool and added later to the body.

(SAN SEVERINA) GLIZA
IRENE SILES

8. Irene Siles

Carmen told us she could produce 15 dolls in one week, and that she usually sold them to a wholesaler who brought them to the Cochabamba and La Paz markets. In the past, Banco Communal loans had helped her considerably, as she was able to purchase the wool, yarn, and dyes for her dolls at a better price by paying directly and therefore gain more profit from her sales. Although she was grateful for the initial boost Freedom from Hunger had given her, she now earned enough to manage on her own. She was doing so well, in fact, that she was even experimenting with new forms, such as large picture-blankets, composed of many 14-inch-square patterned rectangles. She proudly held up some of the completed squares, which I thought were very innovative and beautiful. When I told her how much I liked her work she responded by saying "es por usted" (this is for you) and giving me one of the squares. I hugged her appreciatively. Before we left, Carmen insisted that we all have our picture taken. It was a playful experience, as we stood among the beautiful flowers in her yard, hugging our dolls and wearing the hats she had knitted.

9. Child Nestled in a Carrying Blanket

(VIRGEN DEL CARMEN) GLIZA

10. Spinning Wool

CIRILA ZORITA
(VIRGEN DEL CARMEN) GLIZA

11. Cirilia Zorita Spinning Wool

12. Demetria Guevara Knitting a Chompa

The Celebration

My final afternoon in Cliza was an entertaining one. The Communal Justo Juez had been functioning for four years, and since they were at the end of a loan cycle, it was time to celebrate (Fig. 14). They began with an exuberant throwing of confetti, followed by loud firecrackers. Soon the confetti was brushed off the long table in front of the room, and the women began setting out plates amply filled with corn, potatoes, rice, meat, and salad. This was a special feast to which they had each contributed. Jorge and I were invited to sit at the table and eat. Since the group was large, some women sat on benches placed around the patio, and others sat in chairs or on the ground. Everyone seemed to enjoy the food as well as the chicha (a local, nutritious brew made from fermented corn). Grateful that the loan cycle had been completed and that, with Pachamama's help, their money had multiplied, everyone poured a few drops of chicha on the earth to thank her.

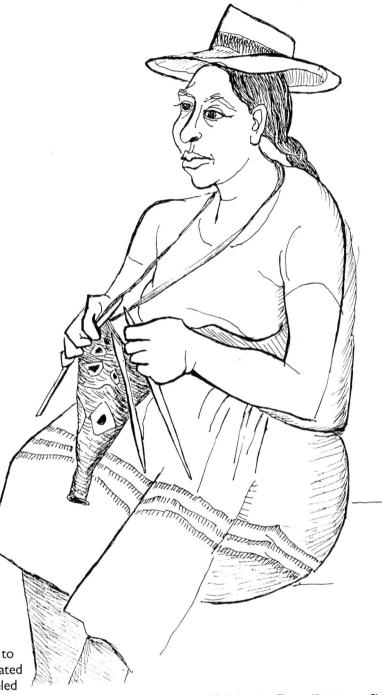

13. Valentina Flores Knitting a Ch'uspa

Anzaldo

The next morning, I awoke early to go with Jorge to Anzaldo, a rural village located many miles from Cochabamba. As we traveled down the dusty mountain roads, the rock-strewn landscape seemed barren of life. But as we came closer, there were clusters of trees and isolated homes constructed from mud and stone and surrounded by long stretches of rock walls. Flocks of lean sheep and goats grazed among the thorny brush. Occasionally their caretakers, young boys, would follow our jeep, frantically hoping we would wave back, and we did.

It was early afternoon when we descended from the mountain and arrived in Anzaldo, a small village consisting of only a few adobe homes. When we got to the Freedom from Hunger office, it was almost an hour before the meeting was to begin, but already several women were waiting for Jorge to open up the doors of the Banco Communal (Figs. 16 and 17). Jorge introduced me to the women. There was a grandmother, her daughter, and several grandchildren. As they sat on the steps of the adjacent building, the grandmother was spinning wool while the daughter and granddaughter knitted. It was wonderful to see three generations of women all working together at the traditional craft of creating *chompas* (sweaters) and *ch'uspas*.

After I sketched the women, we still had some time before the meeting, so Jorge and I went for a short walk. The village had a church, a little park, and a few cobblestone streets, but it felt like a ghost town. The streets were deserted and wooden doors of the homes were closed because most people were still out working on their farms. I was surprised when Jorge took me to a small store located in the middle of town. The store, which was the front room of a home, was so small that both Jorge and I could barely fit in it at the same time, but when we got inside I was amazed to see it cluttered with a wide range of necessary supplies, including bread, pasta, rice, sugar, vegetables, notebooks, medicines, and even nails.

Jorge introduced me to Viviana Alvarez, the storekeeper, an older, stocky woman with many lines on her face. Since the store was so small we stood on the steps outside to talk. I soon learned that Viviana had worked in the store for over 40 years. Her husband had died 12 years ago, and she now managed the store by herself, sometimes working from 6 a.m to 10 p.m. She had nine children, but all had moved away to the city for school or work.

"Even though I miss my children, I don't want to leave," said Viviana. "The store is my life."

Viviana told us that she had the only store in town and she tried to stock a little bit of everything. However, as she got older it was becoming more difficult to travel to Cochabamba to get the supplies. Fortunately, in recent years, with loans from Freedom from Hunger, she could afford to stock more supplies and didn't have to go as often.

Although Jorge and I seemed to be the only ones wearing watches, when we returned to the Banco Communal at 3 p.m. for the meeting, most of the women had already arrived. They sat on benches placed against the wall (Fig. 18). Many looked tired, as they had walked several kilometers from their rural farms. Jorge sat in front of the group with

14. Julia Ramirez and Her Children

GLIZA

15. Cliza Celebration

ANZALADO

16. *Members of the Banco Communal Anzaldo*

the Communal president and, much to my dismay, behind him on the wall was a glossy calendar featuring a slim young woman whose skimpy tee shirt featured a Bolivian beer logo. This free-for-the-asking, sexist poster appeared in many business establishments throughout the Cochabamba area. Unfortunately, in the Freedom from Hunger office it competed with less colorful but more informative posters featuring vital health information. Today, Freedom from Hunger is producing its own calendar that I hope will replace this one.

Anzaldo was one of the newer associations and because Credit with Education was a concept that isolated, rural women required more time to absorb, I admired Jorge as he patiently described and repeated the program goals. The women seemed worried and repeatedly asked what would happen to their savings. He told them over and over that they would have access to their savings at the end of the loan payment. Their money would also accumulate interest and would benefit them in times of food scarcity or family emergency. Gradually they seemed convinced (Fig. 19).

LA PAZ AND LAKE TITICACA

The next day I left Cochabamba for La Paz, where I would spend the final week of my journey visiting the banco communales of the Altiplano region. Although only an hour away by plane, this area was strikingly different than the Cochabamba region. Surrounded by the Andes mountains and windswept plains, the region has a cold climate and its soil is less fertile. The indigenous people struggle to survive.

La Paz itself is a city of many contrasts. Modern high-rise office buildings and hotels stood adjacent to the traditional herbal markets of Linares Street, famous for its many stalls containing herbal remedies, health-promoting teas, good luck charms, and llama fetuses (Figs. 20 and 21). I was fascinated by the indigenous customs related to the fetuses (Fig. 22). The llamas are important in the Altiplano region, as they provide wool and transport for produce. However, in the cold winters, they abort naturally, and their fetuses are collected to fulfill a unique cultural practice that transcends socioeconomic classes. The dried fetuses are buried in the earth, in the foundation of new office buildings or rural adobe homes to encourage and assure health and prosperity to future inhabitants.

My guide in the Altiplano region was Guillermo Alarcon, the La Paz regional director, who was also a local promoter. We were to travel around Lake Titicaca, where 60 Freedom from Hunger groups had been established. Our first destination was the town of Tiquiana, approximately a two-hour drive. And as we drove down the dusty roads close to the lake, I was glad to get to know Guillermo, a tall, slim man with endless energy. He told me he had previously worked

ANZALADO

17. Anzaldo Children

18. Banco Communal Meeting

with Meals For Millions, before the name and program were changed to Freedom from Hunger. In his eight years of experience, he had seen profound changes from a program that imposed the learning of technical skills, most which would not be used after the leadership left or the equipment broke down, to a program based on encouraging people's own self-initiative to make lasting changes. He also remembered when the Credit with Education program had involved men as well as women. According to Guillermo, the men were found to be less reliable; when the program changed to serve women exclusively, the rate of loan repayment rose to 99 percent.

Most of all, Guillermo was proud of the program's education component, which touched upon deeply embedded cultural values, such as machismo.

SEVERINA VALDERRAMA

19. Gradually They Seemed Convinced

"Men always think they know more than women do about everything," said Guillermo, who described machismo as both "physical and verbal violence."

"When the man tells a woman that he beats her just because '*eres mujer*' (just because she is a woman), he puts in the woman's head that she is incapable of achieving. But in reality she is more responsible than the man."

When I asked how the husbands responded to the women's self-initiative, he replied, "At first the husband doesn't want his wife to participate in the banco communales, but when he sees how she contributes more

20. Linares Street Herb Vendors

to the family than he can, and they eat better, the husband gradually undergoes a change in attitude."

After several hours of travel, we crossed the lake by ferry and arrived in the small town of San Pedro, which stretches along the lake on one side and has a small church and several restaurants and stores. Above the cobblestone streets were terraced hills where women grew sustenance crops. Guillermo informed me that this was one of the poorest regions in all of Latin America; the soil was depleted and the villagers survived primarily on potatoes and fish.

Guillermo was warmly greeted by the women when we arrived at the Banco Communal, which was held in the courtyard of a small home. There were over 40 women, some nursing babies and others spinning or knitting. The women were dressed much differently than the women in the Cochabamba region. They had felt bowler hats perched on their heads and wore thick wool shawls and several layers of ankle-length skirts. It was very cold, as the elevation was over 14,500 feet (Fig. 23).

Guillermo explained that the Banco Communal San Pedro Bajo had just completed 11 loan cycles, and the women were holding elections for new officers. Only one woman was running for president, and when the vote was called all the women raised their hands, and she was reelected unanimously.

Although she seemed pleased they had elected her, she somewhat shyly told the group, "To be president is a big responsibility, and it is a big pain for my head. It is difficult for me, as I can't read well, and I have to think carefully before signing the reports. But I will do the best I can."

The promoters assured her they would always be present to assist her.

After election of the other officers, the promoters began to distribute new loans. When all of the women had received their new packet of money, they formed three small groups for the ritual blessing of their money—in the hope that it would multiply. Each group spread a special, woven blanket on the ground and put bright, green coca leaves in the center. Each woman then placed her packet of money around the leaves and poured drops of liquor on the ground to honor Pachamama.

We left before the meeting was over, because it was already late in the afternoon and we were scheduled to attend the Cama Cachi Banco Communal meeting many miles down the road. But along the way we stopped, as Guillermo noticed a Banco Communal member chopping weeds on a small plot next to the road and stopped to greet her. After a brief hello, she continued to work and I was surprised to see her dip her hand into a plastic bag containing a white chemical pesticide, which she sprinkled around each plant. Guillermo explained that in the "green revolution" of the

21. Traditional Herbal Market

22. *Selling Llama Fetuses*

23. *San Pedro Banco Communal*

1960s many chemical company representatives had introduced the use of insecticides and fertilizers. Although in the first few years the crop results were excellent, the harvest yields soon decreased. Meanwhile, the farmers' dependency on chemical consumption, along with debt, had kept increasing.

"*No es bueno* (this is not good)," said Guillermo, acknowledging that chemical dependency was now a common problem.

We arrived too late for the Cami Cachi Communal. The meeting was over and the promoters had left. However, many of the women were still there, and as Guillermo spoke with the president, I began to sketch (Figs. 24 and 25). Much to my surprise, the group treasurer, Zaina Tliullic, had a little pad and she took the initiative of sketching me as I sketched the others. The women gathered around us and laughed at our different results. I was very pleased when Zaina offered me her sketch as a gift. In turn, I promised to send a photocopy of mine to her.

Copacabana

Although it was late, we once again started on our way. The narrow, unpaved road hovered precariously above Lake Titicaca, slowing our progress. It was dark when we finally approached the town of Copacabana, and its lights spread before us like a bright jewel.

MARIA TINTA DE CARILLO Y HUASCAR
CAMA CACHI

24. Cama Cachi Banco Communal

Guillermo suggested we visit the large cathedral dedicated to the Virgin del Carmen, to which many people made annual pilgrimages. The church was filled with worshipers for the evening mass. As we stood in the back, I was mesmerized by the altar containing the life-sized statue of the Virgin. The altar was surrounded by flowers and elaborate gold ornamentation that glittered in the candlelight. The Virgin, renowned for her miraculous healing powers, seemed to project an aura of warmth and hope that embraced without distinction the barefoot poor as well as the upper class.

The next morning, Guillermo attended a 6 a.m. banco communal meeting while I walked around Copacabana. The market was filled with vendors selling fish and vegetables (Fig. 26). There were many stores that featured a variety of traditional carrying blankets and souvenirs. I was particularly interested in the weavings and disappointed that I had not met a weaver from this area.

The Way Back

When Guillermo returned from the meeting, he explained that we would return the same way we had come, but continue on to the village of Chiripaca. There I would meet the promoters Mercedes and Nelson, my guides for the final three days of my trip, in which I would visit the Southern Altiplano region. Guillermo assured me that before we reached our destination, I would get my chance to meet a weaver.

25. *Angelica Chura Spinning Wool*

Midway through our return journey, Guillermo turned down the road to Alto Parqupin, a town high up on a hillside, and in front of her house sat Juana Velasco, a Banco Communal member, weaving a carrying blanket. After Guillermo introduced us, I enjoyed watching her weave. I was interested in the process as well as the result, a blend of vibrant colors and designs. As she sat on the ground in front of her loom, which was approximately four feet wide and hammered into the earth with metal spikes, her deft fingers pushed and pulled the colored wools through the loom's warp. She then pressed the strands tightly together so that I could gradually see the design formation.

As Guillermo spoke with her in Amyra, I began to draw her (Fig. 27). However, I was soon distracted by the sound of music, loud brass trumpets that resounded from the town plaza below us. Guillermo informed us that it was the town's annual celebration, and we decided to drive to the plaza to get a better view. As we got closer, I was stunned by the elaborate, sculpture-like costumes worn by the men as they danced. The costumes reminded me of suits of armor, and Guillermo explained that the dance was an indigenous representation of the Spanish Conquest. Guillermo explained that the villagers saved for a long time to buy the cardboard, fabric, and gold trim used in constructing the costumes, and only wore them on this special occasion. The festival was one of the few escapes from an arduous daily routine.

Chirapaca

By afternoon we arrived at the Chirapaca high school, where the banco communal was in progress. I was immediately overwhelmed by the number of women present. There were, 47 of them, all dressed with heavy wool shawls and long skirts. They sat squeezed into school seats with attached desks (Fig. 28). The promoters, Mercedes and Nelson, were congratulating the group for successfully completing their third loan cycle.

I immediately began to sketch their intense expressions, but before I had time to finish they all got up to go outside for their celebration. It was a stunning sight as the women began spreading their square carrying blankets on the ground, forming one long, colorful chain of inter-connecting patterns. They then sat down opposite each other and each woman added some boiled white or purple freeze-dried potatoes and *tarwi* (large, thick-shelled beans) to the blanket. Some women also added little segments of white goat cheese, while others had brought clay bowls of salsa. A small blanket filled with some food was set aside for the promoters to share, and I was invited to join them. In contrast to the Cochabamba women, who didn't seem to mind my photographs, I was sorry that the Altiplano women always seemed to look down or make sure their faces were hidden (Fig 29).

Mercedes and Nelson

The next day, promptly at 7 a.m., Mercedes and Nelson, my new guides, were waiting for me in front of my hotel. After fighting the La Paz traffic and making a quick stop so Mercedes could purchase food for our trip (*empanadas* and large bottles of soda pop), we soon left the city and began our journey south toward a very remote mountainous region.

We traveled on an old, unpaved, rocky road that wound around a steep mountain. After three hours of bone-jarring bouncing we reached the pinnacle, where we got out of the car and looked look down across the land. I was amazed by the vast,

26. Copacabana Fish Vendor

JUANA VELASCO

ALTO PARQUIPUCIO, COPACABANA

27. *Juana Velasco Weaving a Carrying Blanket*

28. Chripaca

CHIRAPACA

brown, panoramic landscape that spread before us. It seemed barren and void of all signs of life. Three large crosses stood on the hill beside us, and before we left, Mercedes poured *agua fuerte* (hard liquor) around each cross as an offering of thanks to the Virgin and Pachamama for having brought us safely to this point and to ask for continued safe travel.

Over the next three days, we drove many more miles along these rock-strewn roads to some of Freedom from Hunger's most remote banco communales (Fig. 30). As we traveled, I was glad to get to know Mercedes and Nelson. I began to realize that although I was much older than Mercedes, we seemed to have much in common. Like me, she had

29. *Chripaca Banco Communal*

two children, and a very cooperative husband who understood her long days away from home. But what struck me most about Mercedes was the exuberance and excitement she brought to the work and those around her.

Nelson, who was quieter then Mercedes, also had children and a wife who understood his commitment to the process of social change. As a sociology graduate, he had worked with other social agencies before joining Freedom from Hunger.

Both Mercedes and Nelson seemed to have endless energy, and at the various banco communales I really enjoyed observing their interaction. They were a cooperative team and wonderful role models for the women of the banco communales. Their compassion for the women was evident, and it was important for the women to see a man and woman working together as comrades, respectful and supportive of each other.

I soon began to realize that even after eight years, Mercedes continued to thrive as she reached out to connect with people in these remote regions. It was her personal mission to help them combat the extreme deprivation they experienced. Every time we visited a remote village where she could show me a Banco Communal she had helped to establish, she beamed with pride. And as we drove, she was constantly on the lookout for new villages into which Freedom from Hunger could expand.

NAZACARA

30. Nazacara

One afternoon, as we were on our way to the town of Painia Arriba, we saw many men on the roof of an adobe house spreading bundles of straw, while others were lined up passing the straw up to them. Nearby, women chopped lamb meat with axes. Realizing that a banco communal had not been established in this area, Nelson stopped the truck so Mercedes could talk to the people. As the men finished one side of the hut and came down from the roof to take a short rest, Mercedes introduced herself and began to tell them about Freedom from Hunger. One of the men was the village judge, and Mercedes briefly explained to him the basic concepts of Credit with Education. He seemed interested and agreed it would be important for the women to become involved in the project. Before we left, Mercedes arranged a time to meet with the women and explain more about the project.

As we climbed back into the truck to continue our journey, Mercedes was happy. She said this was "*una buena oportunidad,*" and a broad smile spread across her face. This interaction, the spreading of seeds of hope, was just the kind of experience that made it all worthwhile for Mercedes and so many other Freedom from Hunger workers I had met. Although for Mercedes that was perhaps the high point of our journey together, for me it was always the chance to meet an artist or artisan—something which was, in fact, to take place the next day when we reached the isolated town of Iguacuta.

MARTZA Y JIHUACUTA TOMASA TARQUI QUISPE

31. Tomasa Tarqui Guisepe and Grandaughter

32. Cochabamba Market

When we first arrived, the town (which consisted of only of a few rows of adobe homes) seemed deserted except for a dog wandering about. But we stopped at one of the houses where a door was partially open, and I saw Tomasa Tarqui Quispe, a banco communal member, sitting and spinning while talking with her young granddaughter (Fig. 31). She was an older woman and looked worn and tired, but she invited us into her front room, which also served as a store. Mercedes encouraged Tomasa to show me her weavings and soon a wonderful collection was spread before us. I was especially attracted to one carrying cloth composed of a bright blue background interspersed with linear patterns of birds, rabbits, lizards, and flowers.

As Tomasa spoke Aymara, which Mercedes translated, she told us that she had 35 sheep that supplied wool, and it took her at least one month to prepare the wool before she could begin to weave a carrying blanket, which then took two to three months to complete. Her husband did the agricultural work, with which she helped when she wasn't tending their store.

According to Tomasa, the credit-loans had been an impetus for her to keep on weaving because they allowed her to purchase her yarn dyes directly from the supplier at a cost saving. The loans also enabled her to add more inventory to her store, things such as kerosene, candles, soda. But more than anything, the banco communales served as a break from the isolation, a means of building solidarity with other women, and an opportunity to receive health and nutrition education she could share with her daughter and granddaughter.

Tomasa did not have the means to travel regularly to La Paz and usually sold her weavings to an entrepreneur who did. As a result, she did not realize much profit for her effort and seemed very happy to sell me her blue carrying blanket for $35. This was a treasure I have since shared with my students and many others. Tomasa had great pride in her work and it seemed to give a special meaning to her life. However, when we left this bleak village, I couldn't help but regret that Tomasa would probably never receive the financial or professional recognition she deserved for her creativity.

Conclusion

Later that evening, when we returned to La Paz, I said goodbye to Mercedes and Nelson, as I would fly back to Oregon the following day. I was grateful I had traveled far beyond the tourist routes into isolated villages that few visitors ever saw. Although the environment often seemed desolate, there was always more life to ferret out than the closed doorways or empty town plazas suggested at first glance. Mercedes, Nelson, Guillermo, Jorge, and others had opened doors for me so I could see the beauty beyond. I had a better understanding of the work of the promoters and their relentless promotion of women's solidarity. They also encouraged self-worth and the means to overcome machismo. They fervently believed—and knew from experience—that change was possible. All one had to do in order to realize this fact was to see the difference between the women in villages or towns with banco communales and the women who were still isolated and had no sense of future progress.

I was sorry that Tomasa and the other weavers, knitters, and artisans would never know how much their work had inspired me. In my painting Pachamama, New Horizons, which I completed at the journey's end at my Oregon studio, not only did I incorporate the vibrant indigenous love of color and nature, manifested especially in Tomasa's work, but also the impressions I had absorbed throughout my travels in Bolivia (Figs. 32 and 33). The painting's central theme contains my interpretation of Pachamama as she embraces within her body all forms of life, especially children, who in turn tenderly embrace sheep and rabbits. Up above, one of Pachamama's arms extends as a bird form, a symbol of hope, while the other arm holds a symbolic coca leaf containing male and female forms. Pachamama's eyes are wide open, and flying from each of them are pale blue birds with human forms, suggesting liberation of both male and female. An aura of sunshine embraces Pachamama while long, green leaves spiral upward behind her.

33. *Rabbits and Ducks, Cochabamba Market*

My personal Latin American journey had come full circle. It began with my experiences in Mexico with the Otomi Indians and concluded with Bolivia's indigenous Quechua and Amayra peoples. These experiences have expanded my world view to encompass a non-materialistic respect for the earth. This painting was my homage to all indigenous peoples as well as Pachamama. As Mercedes, Nelson, and others had thanked Pachamama by the pouring of *agua fuerte* on the ground, I thanked her by pouring my vision onto the canvas with acrylic paint.

Thailand
Credit Associations and Fieldworkers

In February 1995, I visited Thailand, my third Freedom from Hunger project site. Even though 21 years had elapsed since my first journey to this predominantly Buddhist nation, I still had vivid memories of the ornate Buddhist temples with their larger-than-life statues of Buddha that dominate both the urban and rural landscape (Fig. 1). Trees and plants frequently surrounded the wats, emphasizing the interdependence between the past and the present, nature and people. However, while many aspects of Thailand's ancient cultural heritage remained visible, it became apparent with my first cup of coffee at the airport Burger King that many changes had occurred.

Many new images emerged in my sketchbook as I visited credit associations in Thailand's northeast district of Champuang. There, rainfall was sparse and soil nutrients depleted, but it was encouraging to see the resourcefulness activated by Credit with Education programs, as women participated in traditional activities such as silkworm raising, dry-season gardening, and tobacco processing.

MR. PHONGLIKIT

The Freedom from Hunger coordinator in the Champuang district, Mr Phonglikit Luskanant (the Thai tradition is to address people by their first name), met me at the Nakon airport, about 40 kilometers from Champuang. Mr. Phonglikit, a former school teacher who had also been employed at a United States base in Thailand during the Vietnam War, spoke excellent English. I was grateful, as I only knew a few Thai words. He was a very kind man, and we soon enjoyed talking about our common status as grandparents.

That evening, over a sumptuous Thai dinner at a local restaurant, I learned more about the Freedom from Hunger program in Thailand. Mr. Phonglikit told me that the Credit with Education program had been initiated in 1989 in the Champuang district and had since expanded to three other districts: Roi-et, Udon Thani, and Udon Ratchatkani. At first there was reluctance to borrow money. Women felt that payments on the principal as well as the interest and savings each week would not be possible due to the long duration of their seasonal projects (Fig. 2). Therefore, the program was modified to a six-month loan cycle instead of four, and meetings were held once a month instead of weekly. Only interest and savings were then collected, and the loan was paid back in one "balloon payment" at the end of the cycle. Repayment of loans was 100 percent.

Mr. Phonglikit told me that Credit with Education had been very beneficial, as the savings enabled families to withstand crises such as droughts and protect their futures by diversifying their income-generating projects, combining farming or animal raising with craft production. The education component was also important. Recent surveys showed that participants spent more money than others on food higher in protein and nutritional

1. Seated Buddha

value. And while many mothers had to be educated about the benefits of colostrum, the "first milk" that comes from the breast and is a natural inoculant which protects the newborn from disease, it was heartening to learn that 96 percent of women involved in the program gave their newborns colostrum, as compared to only 64 percent of non-participants (Figs. 3 and 4).

Another Freedom from Hunger goal was achieved in 1992, when a partnership was established with the Foundation for Integrated Agricultural Management (FIAM), a non-government foundation with a long track record of programs designed to improve the lives of the rural poor. FIAM was now in the process of taking over the daily implementation of Credit with Education. This partnership would allow Freedom from Hunger to expand its program to other districts and in other countries.

SPIRITS IN HOUSES AND TREES

The next morning, Mr. Phonglikit picked me up at my hotel to take me to the Freedom from Hunger office. As we drove through Champuang, I noticed how the old and the new co-existed. While there were some modern structures—mostly schools, banks, and government buildings—most of the streets were dusty and unpaved. Cows grazed in empty lots adjacent to restaurants and shops.

As we drove through the center of town, I admired the "spirit houses" that stood in front of every office building, shop, and family home (Fig. 5). They were miniature replicas of Thai homes, elevated chest-high upon a platform supported by sturdy carved posts. Beside the spirit houses were jars with incense sticks and small bowls of offerings that usually contained some grains of rice. When I asked Mr. Phonglikit about them, he told me that they were homes for the ancestor spirits.

"When a family member dies, the spirit leaves the body, and then returns in dreams," said Mr. Phonglikit. "The spirit is disturbed and will say, 'Now I have no home. I have nothing to eat or drink.' So people believe the spirit needs a little home, a place to rest and to receive some incense, flowers, and a little food."

As we continued on our way, we passed several trees which were tied with string and cloth. Mr. Phonglikit pointed out this was another place spirits resided.

"The earth, trees, and water are considered as living, rather than inert entities," said Mr. Phonglikit. "The earth is the mother of us all. When someone thinks a person has done something wrong and the accused tells his accuser, 'I am not guilty,' innocence is proven by swearing before the sky, earth, or a tree."

2. *Credit Payments*

3. Receiving Health Information

Mr. Phonglikit told me the nearby province of Buriram had once been covered with teakwood forests, but the trees were almost all clear-cut and replaced with fast-growing eucalyptus as part of the government's reforestation effort.

A monk, Phra Prajak, had organized the villagers to protest the clear-cutting, and they had tied these white strings around the trees, indicating their sacred status. In spite of government orders, the trees were not cut down. For one year, the Thai government suspended the reforestation program. Ultimately, Phra Prajak was chased away from the forest by government troops, but I, for one, was inspired by this story of resistance.

THE FREEDOM FROM HUNGER OFFICE

The Freedom from Hunger office, which also had a spirit house in front of it, was located in a small residential house shared with the Public Health Department. Mr. Phonglikit's staff consisted of three field workers: Mr. Vira, who had been in the program since 1989 and drove the staff pickup; Hnong, who was new to the program; and Tong, a young woman with a cheerful smile who had just graduated from high school. On the wall of the office was a list of the credit associations in the area, their monthly meeting schedules, and the responsible field workers. There were 42 "*bans*" (villages) in all and according to Mr. Phonglikit the program was growing rapidly.

4. *Receiving Health Information*

BAN KHUNLA KHON

MRS. CHIN
BAN MUANG PHI

5. Spirit House

BAN KSAO

6. *Women Running Their Own Groups*

Tong told me that many techniques had been developed to introduce Credit with Education. One of the most effective of these was a game which used play-money to represent the basic loan, the interest payments, and the savings. Another method was showing the women a slide presentation of established Credit Associations so they could see others like themselves running their own groups and benefitting from hard work (Fig. 6).

BAN PRADOK

At 10:00 a.m. the sun was intense and the temperature approximately 90 degrees when Mr. Phonglikit, Mr. Vira, Tong, and I arrived at the nearby association of Ban Pradok, a small village with traditional homes that stretched out along several lanes. When we entered the compound, some women were seated on the expansive roots of a large, leafy tree, while others were just arriving, pushing their children in two large produce carts that looked like wheelbarrows (Fig. 7).

While the credit association officers, overseen by Tong, called each woman to present her monthly interest payment and savings—a procedure similar to those I had seen in Bolivia, Burkina Faso, and Ghana—I was surprised by the other activities that were occurring simultaneously.

7. Ban Pradok, Waiting for the Meeting to Begin

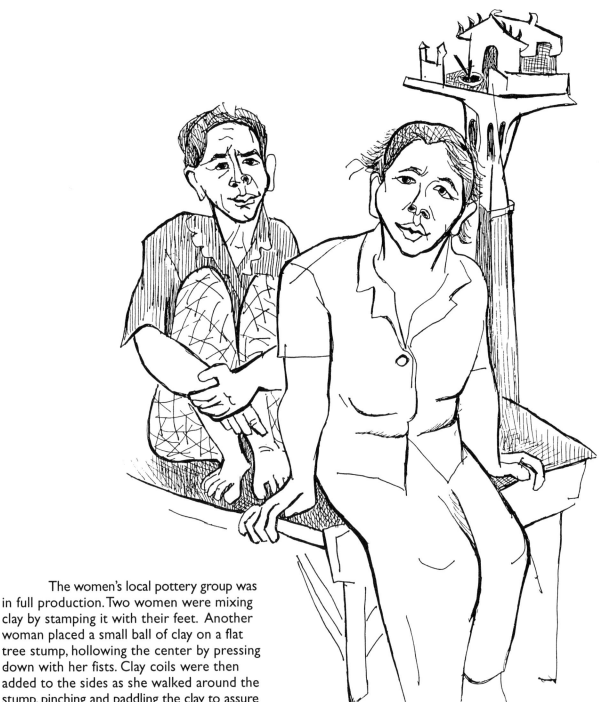

8. Mrs. Veon Phapimai

The women's local pottery group was in full production. Two women were mixing clay by stamping it with their feet. Another woman placed a small ball of clay on a flat tree stump, hollowing the center by pressing down with her fists. Clay coils were then added to the sides as she walked around the stump, pinching and paddling the clay to assure even thickness and symmetry. The women were creating a variety of useful items including food containers, flower pots, and water storage vessels. These clay pots used for water storage were very important. It was customary to offer visitors a cup of water, and the containers could be found at the entrance of every compound.

I was introduced to Tong's mother, Mrs. Phapimai (Fig. 8), the organizer of the group, who told me she received orders for pottery from Khorat, Champuang, and Phimai. She utilized her loan to pay men to carry clay from the nearby pit and to collect wood and straw for the firing so that she and

9. Chickens and Cows

her team of women could focus on production. Mrs. Phapimai said that when a large quantity of a certain form was commissioned, she dispersed the order among several women. "You cannot tell any difference between their pots," she proudly told us, happy that the pottery was as uniform as that which came from a factory.

Pottery was sold on market day, along with produce, grain, cloth, etc., but in recent years it competed with an influx of inexpensive enamel ware. The enamel ware lasted longer and was perceived as a status symbol. Thus, Mrs. Phapimai worried that the younger generation would lose interest in pottery production. She also thought educated women preferred office work.

More than two hours later, after all the credit payments had been made and the meeting came to a close, I was surprised when the women formed a circle and began to sing. As I watched, remembering my Bronx girl scout meetings, they sang several songs with patriotic zeal, concluding with the positive gesture of an upraised fist. Mr. Phonglikit translated the lyrics:

Credit Association members must save money, be orderly, honest, diligent, and faithful. Credit Association members should be strong and maintain themselves and their families in good health.

Over the next few days, as we returned to this district to attend many meetings, I became more familiar with the villages, their amenities and compounds. Most villages have a community meeting center made of a cement foundation and a thatched roof, where Freedom from Hunger members gather. There is usually a small village store, where beer, soda, and packaged foods such as crackers and sweets are sold along with grain and some fresh produce. Sometimes there is even a small restaurant specializing in rice and noodles. In one village, I saw an ice cream vendor who made his rounds by bicycle, pulling a little refrigerator cart behind him.

Homes consist of square, elevated structures usually made of unpainted wood. The family lives above, while underneath there is a shaded patio, which serves as a rest and work area in the daytime and a place to keep animals at night (Fig. 9). During monsoon season, the rains can come in torrents and the patio offers shelter. In the hot, humid weather, it offers protection from the sun and a place to do food processing.

Another standard household feature in this region of scarce rainfall is the huge, cement rain-storage jars. The jars, which are approximately five feet tall, are usually produced in a factory. In the dry season, they provide a family's main water supply; some families, depending on their size and their wealth, possess several. The wealthiest families have a multi-purpose tuktuk, a small, colorfully painted truck that serves either as a vehicle for transportation or as a motor for pumping water.

When I had spare time, I always enjoyed sketching the villagers. The women have short hair and wear western blouses or t-shirts on top of traditional wrap-around skirts made from brightly patterned cloth pulled tight and tucked in at the waist (Fig. 10). The men wear western shirts and pants, but there were very few young men. When I asked Mr. Phonglikit about this, he explained that most men left after the rice harvest to find cash employment in the cities, where they worked in factories or the tourist industries.

According to Mr. Phonglikit, this led to many problems, including the spread of AIDS, as men would often visit prostitutes while they were away and then pass diseases to their wives. Over 10 percent of Thai women between the ages of 15 and 34 are employed in the sex trade.[1] And while Thailand is renowned for its brothels, including those with child prostitutes, Mr. Phonglikit said that most of the prostitutes came from impoverished areas of the northern province, where the young women were very slender and had delicate features as compared with Champuang women, who had stockier builds. According to Mr. Phonglikit, Freedom from Hunger had done a lot

MRS. SUN CHATONGLANG
BAN NONSON

10. Mrs. Sun Chatonglong and Her Son

MR. VICHIT BOONYO-PAKON
BAN PRASUK , CHIEF

11. The Village Chief Seated Beside a Money Tree

12. Ban Prasuk Credit Association Meeting

to minimize the spread of AIDS by disseminating health information as well as encouraging family unity.

BAN PRASUK

One evening at the end of the first week, we traveled to the nearby village of Ban Prasuk to attend a credit association meeting. Many dirt roads extend out from Champuang like the wrinkles and creases of one's palm. And even though this village was only a short distance away, I was amazed Mr. Phonglikit could find his way along the dark, dusty pathways with no signposts or markings.

When we finally arrived at Ban Prasuk, a large, sprawling village, I was surprised to hear the women being summoned to the meeting over a loudspeaker. Mr. Phonglikit explained that the village had acquired electricity six years ago, so now Mr. Vichit Boonyo-Pakon, the village chief (Fig. 11), assembled people by a public address system instead of the traditional drum. In the past, many quick drumbeats indicated that an accident had occurred or that an ox had been stolen, and

MRS. PHIN SAE-JIM
BAN PRASUK

13. Mrs. Phen Sae-Jim

people should come carrying knives or machetes. But a series of calm, regular beats reminded villagers it was time for an assembly, a dance, or a feast.

According to Mr. Phonglikit, the introduction of electricity was a mixed blessing, as it had created a demand for items that most families couldn't afford. Nevertheless, in recent years national banks were authorized to give credit to families that were willing to provide their land deeds as collateral. People bought such items as television sets and cassette players, but if they weren't able to make their payments, they often lost their land.

In a short time, approximately 60 women were assembled in the patio area under the house of the chief (Fig. 12). The chief's wife was the credit association president, but before she spoke the chief welcomed me and in turn asked me to greet the group. Mr. Phonglikit translated as I told the women how impressed I was by their organization, solidarity, and commitment to personal change through education and hard work. The women politely applauded. Before I sat down, the chief asked Mr. Phonglikit if he could ask me a personal question. He wanted to know if I was married, and if so, how many children I had. When I responded that I was not only married but had grandchildren, I received an extra-loud round of applause. Their reaction made me realize how important children were in village life and how the more children a woman had, the higher the social status she was accorded.

The meeting was conducted in the same manner I had seen before, but I was surprised when it ended without a health education segment. When I asked Mr. Phonglikit about this, he told me that since the program was in a transitional phase between FIAM and Freedom from Hunger, the focus was on economics rather than health. Before we left, the chief, who had seemed pleased with my answers to his questions, invited us to return the following day for a tour of the diverse economic activities of Credit Association members.

The next morning, en route to Ban Prasuk, I saw a house with many cows peering out from a fenced patio, and we stopped the car to take a closer look. A small, elderly woman was sitting beside the house, and I became excited when I realized she had a pet monkey. As she held the monkey in her lap like a small child, she told us her name was Mrs. Sai Prue-Ngan and that her children had bought the monkey to keep her company while they were away working. The cows she had inherited from her mother. Mrs. Prue-Ngan told us she was 67 years old but in good health except for missing many teeth. The loss of her teeth, however, did not keep her from masticating betel nut, as her lips were a deep red color from its potent juice.

When we arrived at Ban Prasuk, the chief was once again talking on the loudspeaker. This time he was summoning people to come and contribute money for the completion of a new *wat*. Nearby, an old woman was resting on a bamboo bed in the shade of her patio. Curled up in a fetal position, she seemed oblivious to the chief's loudspeaker. I soon learned that the woman was over 100 years old.

After the chief was able to turn his fundraising effort over to an assistant, he took us around the village and introduced us to several women involved with the credit association. The first was Mrs. Phin Sae-Jim (Fig. 13), an older, very proud-looking woman I recognized from the meeting the night before. When I asked her how she used her Freedom from Hunger loans, she

14. Contented Pigs

15. Rice-Noodle Vendor

told me she raised pigs (Fig. 14) and that it was her main income source. She was a widow, but had seven children, all of whom had left the village. Through the credit association, she managed to save 100 *baht* per month (25 *baht* equals approximately one U.S. dollar).

Next, the chief thought I would enjoy meeting Mrs. Somkuan Siwachatmethi, who has a rice-noodle business. It was a short walk through the village to her home, and as we made our way, I observed compounds of distinct economic levels and varied resources. While most homes are constructed of wood and have only wooden window shutters and corrugated metal roofs, there were a few homes made of bricks and mortar that had glass windows and tiled roofs. While some families have only a few chickens or one or two lean cows in their fenced compound, others have colorfully painted *tuktuks*.

Mrs. Somkuan, a short, plump woman, welcomed us when we arrived at her home and then led us to her patio, where her noodle-making enterprise was in full swing. She explained that she and her two friends began early each morning by mixing and kneading rice flour into a pliable consistency. The dough was then placed in a can with perforated round holes in the bottom. The rice dough was gradually pushed through the holes in a little hand-held lid until long strands fell into a large pot of boiling water. After several minutes of cooking, the

16. Mrs. Tuam Boontaen and Family

BAN NONGWA

17. Boiling the Silk Cocoons

noodles were taken out, rinsed, and placed in a bamboo basket that was lined with bright green palm leaves. By noon, Mrs. Somkuan was ready to walk door-to-door selling her noodles. It was her daily routine, and she had many steady customers. To make her deliveries, she carried two baskets suspended from a bamboo pole which rested on her shoulders. One basket contained her noodles. In the other basket she carried a covered pot of meat sauce, condiments, spoons, and bowls (Fig. 15).

Mrs. Somkuan told us she was a widow and supported herself and one daughter, who was studying nursing. The chief joked (or perhaps he really meant it!) that since there were 20 to 30 widows in Ban Prasuk, he was planning a contest for widows and asked if I would return again to be the judge. The criteria for selecting the winner would be professional status (how much money they earned), moral behavior, physical attributes, and whether they were good mothers to their children and good role models for others. I wondered (but didn't ask) whether he would apply the same standards to men whose wives had died.

After a noodle lunch purchased from Mrs. Somkuan, the chief took me to meet Mrs. Ruam Boontaen and her husband, Tai, who were vegetable gardeners. After meeting them at their home, we accompanied them a short distance to their vegetable garden, which consisted of a verdant medley of

BAN NONGWA

18. Spinning Silk Thread

eggplants, onions, beans, lettuce, peppermint, peanuts, and tomatoes, all growing in orderly rows. The garden looked well weeded and watered, and Mrs. Tuam said they used only natural fertilizers, which they bought from people who had animals. She also told us that she had been a credit association member for only three years but her savings were substantial, approximately 7,500 *baht*. Her goal was to save 30,000 *baht* so she and her husband could invest in a *tuktuk* or a water pump and pipes to install an irrigation system. In addition to growing vegetables in the dry season, they planted seven hectares of rice in the rainy season. This was more than enough to sustain their family, so they sold the surplus to the village store. When I asked this couple if I might draw them, their daughter stood proudly between them; all three appeared lean and strong, with hands not used to being idle (Fig 16).

The chief then gave us a tour of an extensive compound that contained an old residence for monks and the new, ornate *wat* for which he had been collecting money. The *wat* had a bright orange tiled roof, which was bordered with flame-like wood decorations. Several men sat nearby, under the shade of a tree, carving intricately detailed wall panels to complete this temple.

Behind the *wat* was a small, ornate building with a very tall smokestack. I was told this was the crematorium. After cremation, the ashes were placed in clay urns in openings around the *wat* wall or in small, pyramidal shaped *stupas* designed for holding the urns. The openings were then cemented over, and photographs of the deceased person sometimes appeared on the narrow *stupa* shelf, along with flowers, incense sticks, and small bowls of rice as a sign of respect.

SILK: FROM WORMS TO CLOTH

For many years, I had been curious about the production of silk. Before my first trip to Thailand, I remembered learning that Jacqueline Kennedy had traveled there in search of silk cloth for her wardrobe. She was also featured in popular magazines, seated in a canal boat surrounded by other boats carrying vendors and their merchandise, as she made her selection from a variety of beautiful solid, ikat-dyed, and patterned cloth. Her fashion interests brought world attention to an ancient technology unknown to most Americans with Sears-Roebuck budgets, but I regretted that we learned little about the village women who produced the silk.

When I told Mr. Phonglikit about my interest in silk, I was surprised that even though he had grown up in a province noted for silk, he didn't know much about the process. "It is a women's cottage industry; I never really paid attention to it," he said. However, he was aware of commercial factories where silkworms were raised and silk cloth mass produced. Even though I wanted to visit a factory, I wanted most of all to see the process in the more intimate setting of the villages, where it had been done for centuries. Mr. Phonglikit was happy to oblige, and over the next few days we saw many stages of this unique and complicated process performed by credit association members. From the worm to the loom, it was an exciting adventure for both of us.

Because it was dry season and there was little water for the mulberry plants, which are vital in the silk producing process, Mr. Phonglikit had to ask around for several days to find where the process was still being done. Finally, Mr. Phonglikit took me to a nearby village of Ban Nongwa. Our first stop was the home of Mrs. Ghan Kruadno, who had several mulberry plants around the outside of her house. After she greeted us, she took us to a small room in the patio of her house that was set aside for silk worm cultivation. The room had many shelves with large, circular bamboo trays. She pulled out a tray and I could see it contained a mass of squirming, light gray worms. The worms were interspersed

MRS. SIMPLEE NAEBKLANG- BAN PRASAT

19. Knotting the Warp Threads

MRS. SONG UPARACHANG

20. Basket Weaving

MRS. TIP SANINTAR
BAN PAPHUM

21. Mrs. Song Uparachang Weaving a Basket

with dark green mulberry leaves, which they were in the process of decimating. She scooped up a handful of undulating worms so I could observe them more closely. Mrs. Kruadno told us the worms feed on the mulberry leaves for 25 to 28 days before spinning their cocoons. It took another three days for the formation of the silk cocoon. After covering the worms with cheese cloth and carrying the tray on her head to replace it on a high shelf, she took out another tray. This one was filled with the bright yellow, mature cocoons.

After leaving Mrs. Kruadno's compound, we walked through the village, where we were able to see the next step in the silk-formation process. A woman sitting under a tree beside a charcoal stove was patiently taking the mature, yellow cocoons from her bamboo tray and placing them into a pot of boiling water (Fig. 17). The pot had a vertical handle with a small reel attached to the top. After a few minutes, I learned what it was used for. Using a bamboo ladle, she lifted the cocoons out of the water one at a time, loosened their thread, and guided it over the wheel. As she turned the handle on the pot, the silk unwound from the cocoon and fell into a metal container beside her feet. I was amazed when she told us that one little cocoon could produce a thread that stretched over 1.5 kilometers. But it took many worms—approximately 700—and 15 kilograms of mulberry leaves to produce sufficient silk to make one long-sleeved blouse. The silk thread in the bucket was a bright yellow color, but the women told us that when it was rinsed the thread turned a soft white. After all the silk had been removed, only the shriveled worms were left in the boiling water. The women brought us several tiny worms on a plate so we could try this Thai delicacy. Although I declined, Mr. Phonglikit seemed to enjoy this snack. "They are a delicious source of protein," he said, eating them the way an American would munch on a pretzel.

Later that afternoon, we were taken to yet another compound to see the next step in the process: the preparation of the silk for the loom. When we arrived at the compound, an elegant older woman with long, gray hair knotted in a bun was seated on a mat between two spinning wheels. One was a small, wooden wheel with thick spokes and the other was a tall wheel that had long, gracefully carved spokes. She patiently guided the thread from the large wheel to the smaller wheel, in the process spinning the coarse silk into a thin, fine thread ready to weave on the

22. Stringing Tobacco Leaves

MRS. WANDEE LAONGEGG.
BAN PAPHUM

23. Mrs. Wandu Laongegg Resting at Her Loom

loom (Fig. 18). This was a difficult process because the thread kept breaking, and she continually had to reconnect it by twisting the ends together. Although there was a lot of activity around her, she seemed oblivious to everything as she focused on her spinning. As I watched her, a feeling of timelessness came over me as I realized that silk spinning had been done this way for thousands of years.

The next day, Mr. Phonglikit invited me to join him on a visit to several regional villages, and as we walked around the village of Ban Prasat, I was pleasantly surprised to see the final process in the production of silk cloth. As we approached one compound, Mrs. Simplee Nabklang, a credit association member, was seated in her patio at a large, cage-like loom. Her husband sat nearby in a bamboo chair, rocking their sleeping grandchild in a hammock. Mrs. Simplee was weaving a long shawl composed of a vibrant magenta and deep purple pattern, and she didn't seem to mind as we watched and asked questions. The shawl she was creating was very beautiful, and I wanted to purchase one like it. Fortunately, she had already completed one, but she told us it would take her about half an hour to tie and knot the warp threads on either end of the fabric. I did not mind, as it gave me the opportunity to sketch her and learn more about her life (Fig. 19).

Mrs. Simplee told us she was 47 years old and had four children. Previously, she had only woven straw mats, which are coarser and less complicated to weave. I admired her initiative, as she explained that she had learned how to create complex silk patterns by purchasing a weaving from a friend and using it as a model. She told us that after the loom was threaded, it took her approximately four days to complete a cloth. Her weaving was seasonal, so she also worked with her husband on the family farm. However, weaving was important because it provided the family's main cash income.

That evening as we left Ban Prasat, I was grateful for Mr. Phonglikit's effort to show me the complete cycle of silk—from the worm to the loom. I was pleased that silk production had remained an important cottage industry and that it was now encouraged by women's participation in Freedom from Hunger. Many women now used their credit to buy commercial dyes for the silk thread or insecticide for their mulberry plants. Though I would enjoy wearing Mrs. Simplee's silk shawl, it would be even more exciting to show it to my students in my Art and Third World Culture class at Southern Oregon State College.

MRS. YAM KAWDONLE
BAN MUANG PHI

24. Mrs. Yam Kawdonle, a Tired Grandmother

BASKET WEAVING AND TOBACCO PROCESSING

The next night, I was startled to receive a 4:00 a.m. telephone call from Mr. Phonglikit, informing me that his mother-in-law had just died. Although family obligations required him to leave for his home in Bangkok, he told me that Tong, Mr. Vira, and Hnong were all very concerned that I continue with my sketching and photo documentation, and that I should continue to have a "happy experience." Unfortunately, in Phonglikit's absence I would have to rely on my guidebook phrases, as he was the only staff member who spoke English.

Mr. Phonglikit had been a congenial guide and good friend, and I would really miss his personal insights and anecdotes, as they had enriched my understanding of Thailand's history and culture, as well as its present needs.

Before Mr. Phonglikit's departure, he informed the FIAM staff at Roi-et about my sketchbook project and my appreciation of the work of traditional artisans. Therefore, the next day Mr. Vira took me as scheduled to the FIAM headquarters to meet the regional coordinator, Mr. Nawin Kotano, who would then take me to several villages where I could see the local craft of basket weaving.

After a four-hour drive, we arrived at the FIAM office, located in a small building near the center of town. Mr. Nawin was a slender man with a warm smile, and I was relieved that he spoke English. He suggested that, before going to the villages, we should see "Roi-et's most famous *wat*." After a short drive through Roi-et, a city much larger than Champuang, we arrived at the *wat*, and I was surprised to see an immense, gold-plated Buddha standing above the compound. It was at least 120 feet high, and with one hand upraised in a traditional pose, it seemed to calmly monitor the traffic that surrounded the compound.

The compound bustled with activity. It contained a primary school, a religious training center for monks, a souvenir shop, and an impressively decorated *wat* that many tourists came to see. The exterior of the *wat* was covered with intricately carved red and white ornamentation and had a large stairway leading to an ornate doorway, which was guarded by two *nagas* (guardian snakes) with ferocious open jaws. Their detailed, scaly forms contrasted with the slim, graceful lines of the gold-plated Buddha. Many visitors wandered about, and there were benches for resting or meditation. In contrast to the spiritual atmosphere of the *wat*, we ate our

25. Ban Muang Phi, Resident Monk

MRS. KAT KANGKAT
BAN PALAI

26. Raising Ducks

27. Ban Phimai Street Market

lunch a few blocks away at a Thai version of McDonald's which had, instead of hamburgers, rice noodles with variously flavored meat and vegetable broths.

After lunch, we traveled to the village of Ban Papaphum, renowned for its basket weaving. As we walked down the center lane, I noticed most homes had piles of baskets on their patios. Many of these were unfinished, and they reminded me of giant sunflowers because the spokes, which would become the sides of the basket, radiated out from their flat bases (Fig. 20).

At one compound, I was introduced to Mrs. Song Uparachong, a credit association member, who sat in her patio weaving the basket sides. Though I was familiar with the process, since baskets fulfill utilitarian needs in agricultural communities throughout the world, I was surprised by an unusual wooden support system that she used. It consisted of a curved log, approximately 30 inches tall, that was anchored into the ground. Inserted over the log was a solid wood form the size and shape of the basket, which allowed Mrs. Song to rotate the basket as she was making it and maintain a consistent shape (Fig. 21). Nearby, an old man was splitting the bamboo for her to use. Mrs. Song showed me several finished baskets, which had handles and were lacquered. She was delighted when I bought one to bring back with me to the United States.

As we continued our walk through Ban Papaphum, I noticed many large wooden frames leaning against the walls and fences of the compounds. The frames had rows of long strings nailed to them, and I was told that the withered, broth leaves that were strung through them were tobacco leaves in various stages of drying. A short time later, we came to a compound where many women were seated on mats around a huge pile of bright green tobacco leaves that contrasted beautifully with the red patterns of the women's skirts and blouses. Several generations of women worked together, using long iron needles and coarse thread to string the leaves and then attach them to the frames (Fig. 22). As they worked, some women rocked their infants, suspended beside them in cloth hammocks, while others attended to young children or shooed trespassing chickens away. When Mr. Hawin explained that I was a visiting artist representing Freedom from Hunger, the women did not seem to mind that I sketched them. Mr. Nawin told me that, although the Roi-et district, like Champuang, suffered from irregular or unpredictable rainfall, this had been a particularly good year and the tobacco harvest had been better than usual.

We spent the remainder of the day driving to several other villages where I also observed similar basket-weaving and tobacco-processing activities. I enjoyed noticing that, while people were productive and concentrated on their activities, they were able to talk and move about as necessary. Working at home seemed humane compared to the robot-like factory production so many others were forced into in order to earn a cash income (Fig. 23).

28. Pig Head

PHIMAI

29. Fish, Eels, and Snakes

VISITS TO BAN MUANG, NONGJIK, SAMRONG, MUANG PHI, NONSOON, AND YAI PHA

After the Roi-et visit, I realized I had just four days until I would return to Bangkok and then to Oregon. At first, I thought I would not be interested in continuing to attend all the scheduled credit association meetings, as I had seen the routine many times, but I was mistaken. Each village seemed to offer a new cultural perspective, as well as an understanding of Freedom from Hunger's role. However, sometimes I just enjoyed randomly walking about, observing and recording people's activities and expressions.

At Ban Muang Phi, I drew a woman who seemed tired and worn (Fig. 24), while nearby elementary school children, dressed in blue and white uniforms, enthusiastically saluted the national flag before their classes began. The village *wat* was an unpainted wood structure, and I was delighted that one of the two resident monks allowed me to draw him (Fig. 25). I also photographed the local transportation, a little three-wheeled vehicle with benches and a covered top that was cheerfully painted with red, white, and blue designs.

At Ban Samrong, Mrs. Udom Jang Pho, an association member, was very proud to show us how she forged metal into knives and other functional tools. She was one of the few women who had learned this skill from her husband, and they worked together.

At Ban Nonsoon, I noticed women carrying baskets of sugar cane stuffed with cinnamon flavored rice, which they sold en route to their credit association meeting. This village also had a large, elaborate *wat* that was being decorated with strings of lights to embellish it for an upcoming festival. The *tuktuk* passing the *wat* was also decoratively painted, and together their colors were dazzling, and in sharp contrast with the unpainted village homes and the parched land surrounding the village.

At Ban Yai-Pha, the credit association president, Mrs. Yai Sae-ue, took us to her home, where she proudly showed us the pigs she raised and explained how she processed wood into charcoal.

At Ban Palai, a credit association member took us to see her ducks (Fig. 26). Over 50 ducks were waddling about beside a stream, while the woman's husband and her two young sons greeted us from a small bamboo-and-thatch shelter where they slept in order to guard the duck eggs.

THE MARKETPLACE

I decided to dedicate my last day in the Champuang area to one of my favorite activities: market sketching. I chose the nearby town of Ban Phimai because I was told it had both an enclosed indoor market and a bustling outdoor, afternoon market—I was not disappointed.

Early in the morning as I walked along the street leading to the market, there were so many vibrantly striped beach umbrellas on top of the fresh fruit and vegetable stands, I thought I was in New York's Coney Island—a source of memorable entertainment during my youth. I enjoyed sketching women with shopping bags, vendors with broad-brimmed straw hats, and pyramids of produce displayed on wooden tables (Fig. 27). This was not a carnival, just everyday life, hardly comparable to the sterility of a U.S. market, where one pushes a cart filled with frozen and canned goods up to the computerized check-out counter.

My sketching venture continued in the indoor market at the meat stands, where I stopped to look at the jowly, severed

30. Fish Vendors

head of pig sitting on a wooden counter (Fig. 28). Perhaps it was one of the pigs I had seen at the Credit Association member's farm? I did not know, but with little, sharp teeth it grimaced almost humorously at customers as if to remind us all of our mortality. But the pig's smile seemed to say to me, "We should live to the fullest within our means, and enjoy all we can."

At the fresh fish displays, there were eels and snakes in large, water-filled pans. I had to draw them, as well as the young women vendors who sat beside the pans on low benches ready to lift out a selected specimen for a customer (Fig. 29). They would place this squirming merchandise into a plastic bag with water so it would be as fresh as possible after the customer's walk home on this hot day. Meanwhile, between sales, the women's little compacts would come out of their pockets and lipstick would be added to their shapely lips.

Towards evening, the street along the park became even more filled with activity. Vendors began to arrive with baskets filled with an extraordinary array of cooked foods. Dinner customers would buy the food to carry home or eat at benches and tables set up in the street or the park. Once again, this was a festive, happy atmosphere. I particularly liked sketching the vendors who had baskets of smoked fish. The fish were strung together by their heads with cords of bamboo and arranged in circular trays like beaded necklaces (Figs. 30 and 31).

CONCLUSION

As I returned to my home in Oregon, I felt as though I brought with me a blend of new and old impressions created from the 20-year span between my visits. As in the past, people were forced to leave the villages for basic survival because the climate was arid and rainfall unpredictable. But now, with the influx of electricity, people also left so they could get cash incomes to purchase electronic goods such as refrigerators and televisions. Family stability often suffered.

However, despite the pressure for modernization, there was still a respect for the earth and the ancestor spirits. Even in the larger towns and cities, spirit houses abounded, providing a place where people could leave offerings or just admire the life-affirming plants. In 1974, these spirit houses had impressed me so much that, after returning from my journey, I had painted my own version of a spirit house. At that time, my son Jason was four years old, and I portrayed myself as a guardian bird protecting him as I hovered over a spirit house that contained a bird, a symbol of our linked spirits.

For the Thai people, it was also a linking of spirits, past and present, that was protecting them. Through the veneration of the ancestor spirit, traditional values and activities were preserved. This process was facilitated by Freedom from Hunger, which augmented women's income-earning capacity and encouraged them to do projects based on their own cultural traditions and environmental resources. This promoted family and community cohesion, as well as cultural continuity.

Two decades earlier, Jacqueline Kennedy had opened the door to Thailand's aesthetic heritage, exemplified by silk. In 1995, as I returned from my second trip, it seemed appropriate that Hillary Clinton and her daughter Chelsea were returning to this area for a different reason: to emphasize the importance of educating women and to make the U.S. more sensitive to women's contributions to the local economy. Yes, many things had changed in Thailand, but some transitions were positive, as women were coming together to receive education and unite in their struggle for a healthier and better future for themselves and their families.

31. Fish and Vegetable Vendors

[1] Bishop & Robinson, Book Review, *Z Magazine*, Sept. 1995, pg 66-68

5 **THE UNITED STATES:** Georgia, Alabama, and Mississippi Community Health Advisor Networks

My final Freedom From Hunger journey was in the United States, where I traveled to the deep south to visit Georgia, Alabama, and Mississippi. This was a very special trip for me, as—42 years earlier, at the age of 18—I had begun my custom of sketchbook journeys in this same area. Preparing for my 1995 trip, I began to reflect back. I remembered my earlier venture as exciting but also very shocking as I became aware of deeply ingrained racism towards African Americans.

In 1995 I was returning to the South, still carrying a sketch book, but in a professional capacity, to document community health programs that would have been unimaginable 42 years before. However, I would once again be shocked. While some progress had been made, almost half of the Southern population still lived in Third World conditions. And while the Civil Rights struggle had brought about some advances in the social and political life of black Americans, racism and economic exploitation continued to obstruct their hopes and dreams.

THE SOUTH, 1951

In 1951, I had just completed my first year in college, and I was eager to see and explore the United States. Inspired by Mark Twain's *Life on the Mississippi*, Howard Fast's *Freedom Road*, and Langston Hughes' poetry, I set out for the Mississippi River with only seventeen dollars, a small suitcase, and my sketch book. After hitchhiking to St Louis I found a boat going to New Orleans, and the captain agreed to take me along.

Life on the Tradewinds is always interesting. Sometimes I hear the strum of the guitar and harmonica blending fast southern tunes. When the deckhands are not doing their work, they play cards, drink coffee, and talk. Often I get angry as I hear them say "nigger, money tight Jew, and communist," but the steady hum of the boat engine pacifies me.

After three days we arrived at Cairo, Illinois, but a rainstorm delayed our departure, and I decided to leave the *Tradewinds* and hitchhike to Memphis, Tennessee. After arriving in Memphis I stayed the night in the Salvation Army for one dollar.

So, I'm in the heart of the South, where every Negro is a "nigger" who knows his place or is taught it quickly.... I hold my breath and listen, wondering why do people think and talk this way, and how is it possible for this to change.

The next morning I joined the day laborers in the Memphis cotton fields. But my day was shortened by the plantation owner who could not comprehend why a young white woman wanted to hoe cotton.

GAINESVILLE, ALABAMA
CON AGRA

1. Chicken Processing

I worked in the cotton fields today for two hours. The sun was hot but I worked at my own pace and received two dollars. The Negroes worked side by side in long rows, all keeping an equal pace for 10 hot hours. For their sweat and toil they each receive four dollars.

The suntan I got working in the cotton field inadvertently led me to my next adventure on Memphis' Beale Street, where white people usually didn't walk after 5 p.m.

I'm considered a Negro, and a pretty one. At first I didn't know. I walked into a cafe to get a cup of coffee and listen to some jazz records....all the while I think I'm white, they think I'm black.. What goes? Then I begin to catch on.... I am considered a light complexioned Negro.

The realization that I could pass as black opened up a new world of experiences for me. For the rest of the summer, I kept my name as Betty Bernstein and told only one untruth, that I was from a mixed marriage and that my mother was black. I rode in the backs of buses and used public facilities marked for blacks. It was an exciting but lonely time, as I experienced some of the restrictions blacks faced in a white-dominated society.

THE SOUTH, 1995

My 1995 trip began in Atlanta, Georgia, where I met my traveling partner, Elaine Rickets, who was Freedom from Hunger's Marketing and Development Coordinator in the southern United States. We met for the first time at the Atlanta airport, but after four days and 1500 miles of driving in her red, rented car, we would feel as if we had known each other a long time. We visited Freedom From Hunger project sites in Georgia, Alabama, and Mississippi, and met with people in small towns and rural areas where poverty and malnutrition were deeply entrenched. I was well aware of the statistics, but now the numbers were connected with living faces.

Our first stop was Gainesville, Georgia, a two-hour drive. Along the way I had the opportunity to learn more about Elaine's background. She told me that she had always enjoyed being around people and food. While in college she had worked summers as a Chicago fishmonger. After graduating, she taught high school home economics and then became a nutrition consultant for the Beech Nut Nutrition Corporation. Gradually her interests changed and she enrolled in Tulane University's School of Public Health. After graduating in 1994, Elaine came to work for Freedom from Hunger, where she was now coordinator for a four-state program based in Jackson, Mississippi.

Elaine told me that Freedom from Hunger functioned much differently in the United States than it did in the other countries. Rather than Credit Associations and Credit with Education, the programs had evolved as a system of Community Health Advisor Networks (CHANS). The CHANS were based upon recruiting and training volunteers or "natural helpers" who would seek to improve individual and community health by identifying health problems; organizing self-help action in their communities; linking people in need with available health services; and giving advice and assistance to neighbors, friends, and families.

MC DONALDS
Batesville, Mississippi

2. Breakfast at McDonalds

GAINESVILLE, GEORGIA

Gainesville, Georgia, is the self-proclaimed "chicken capital" of the United States. Previously the town had been composed primarily of white, middle-class people, but that was rapidly changing. Since the 1980s there had been a massive influx of immigrants from Mexico and Latin American. Population statistics for immigrants ranged from 20,000 to 50,000, and many people were employed by the numerous poultry-processing corporations, where the work was numbing of body and spirit and low in pay (Fig. 1).

The main road through Gainesville was indistinguishable from most large American towns. It was bordered with gas stations, fast food restaurants, and a few main stores (Fig. 2). There were also many tree-lined neighborhoods of pleasant family homes. However, as we drove around some of the back roads, Elaine pointed out, crowded trailer courts, small wood houses, and two-story brick government apartments—devoid of plants, flowers, or vegetable gardens—where most immigrants lived.

According to Elaine, most of the settled immigrants did not have transportation, or child-care facilities. They also did not speak English and as a result they were seldom aware of the community health and social service programs available to them. While their labor was a valuable commodity, the quality of their lives was often not considered. It was sad to realize that chickens, which scampered about freely throughout most of the rural areas I had visited in my other Freedom from Hunger journeys, were not seen in anyone's backyard in Gainesville, Georgia, "chicken capital of the world."

At Gainesville's Freedom from Hunger office, located in the Public Health Department, we were met by Annalise Blomgren, a program facilitator who had formerly worked as a Peace Corps volunteer in Costa Rica. She told us that for the past two months she had been contacting professional health workers, church leaders, prominent business people, and social service representatives to explain how the CHAN program functioned and ask if they would serve as steering committee members and program advisors. After contacting Human Resources Managers at all the poultry processing corporations, Annalise finally received one affirmative response from Con Agra's Jim Rutledge, and his assistant, Tony Rodriguez. They were interested in cooperating with her and participating in the CHAN program. At the time of our visit, Con Agra had been involved in the CHAN program for almost a month. Annalise had arranged for us to meet with Jim and Tony as well as have a tour of Con Agra.

Con Agra

The Con Agra plant consisted of a series of large windowless concrete buildings surrounded by asphalt parking lots. However, our meeting took place in Jim's office in a small adjacent building that had air conditioning and many windows, allowing his green office plants to flourish. As Jim sat behind a neatly organized desk with Tony seated near him, he told us that Con Agra had branches in nine states and locally employed 600 people for each of their two shifts. An additional 50 people were employed just to clean the machinery.

Jim and Tony said they were glad to be involved with the

3. *Incessant Noise of the Machinery*

CHAN program because they were concerned with keeping workers happy. The Con Agra plant had an annual 50 to 60 percent turnover rate. They also wanted to keep Con Agra's worker compensation payments down by preventing injury and sickness, and addressing other related needs. They felt workers would trust other workers who were Community Health Advisors more readily than management. "As a Christian, it is my personal mission to do what the Bible says about taking care of aliens in our land," said Jim, who seemed sincere in his desire to help people. "The right thing to do is to make better citizens of our employees and make us [citizens] better able to accept them [immigrants]."

Tony agreed, "It is very important for Hispanic employees to become integrated into this community. They need to learn about the health care and other community services available to them here, rather than returning to Mexico when they're sick."

Tony also said learning English was very important, as they also needed to know practical things like their civil rights and what to do when a policeman stopped them. Tony was very pleased that Con Agra had already initiated a GED program and English as a Second Language program in both Spanish and English. There was also a "work site wellness program" led by a staff nurse, who regularly screened employees for hearing loss and high blood pressure. She also produced a health newsletter and initiated health fairs.

Annalise, Tony, and Jim were happy with the progress that had been made since the CHAN system had been initiated at Con Agra. Already 50 potential CHAs had been identified. Although only 17 of these came to their first meeting, Annalise was encouraged by their enthusiastic discussion and commitment to begin the 30-hour training program; three hours per one evening per week for 10 weeks.

"Building trust among low-income, disenfranchised, and frequently illiterate people is slow and difficult work," said Annalise. "The only tangible thing the CHAs receive from their participation is a graduation ceremony, but they begin to realize that knowledge is powerful."

During their first meeting, the CHAs decided that violence, drug abuse, alcohol abuse, and domestic violence were the most important topics for future training sessions: "The first step is to discuss what are the root causes of their mental and physical ailments," said Annalise. "Then we ask them to consider what we can do about these problems."

According to Annalise, ergonomics (human engineering), although cost-effective, is the root of many physical and mental problems. Most work is done in a very solitary atmosphere where there is little contact between people. It is also difficult to adapt to the repeat-motion and monotony of the machine-driven chicken-processing operation. I sympathized as I thought of my mother's 30-year working career in a pocketbook factory and the aches and pains in her fingers and hands as she sat all day long at a sewing machine doing "piece work."

Con Agra Tour

Soon we began our hour-long Con Agra tour in which we entered into a surrealistically white, sterile environment where human identity—i.e., one's face—was hardly visible. Workers were covered with white hairnets and white coats, and rubber

4. *The Killing Room*

5. *A Quick Rite of Passage*

aprons and boots. They wore long, lime-green gloves that made their hands seem claw-like. They also wore ear plugs to block out the incessant noise of the machinery (Fig. 3).

The plant was composed of a series of connecting buildings that separated the different aspects of the process. In one section the killing, depluming, and evisceration took place (Fig. 4). In another, the chicken was chopped into usable and disposable body parts. And in a final area the chicken was packaged and then frozen. The odor in certain parts of the plant was overwhelming, although enormous quantities of water was used at the work stations for cleansing and washing away blood.

Jim and Tony told us that at Con Agra's nearby ranches, 1.25 million chickens were raised to maturity each week. It takes three hours from their chirping entry into the plant until they were ready for the supermarket freezers. Each week, Con Agra processed four million pounds of poultry meat from this plant, and each worker handled approximately 70 birds per-minute in this quick rite of passage.

I was intrigued by the assembly lines which went from one side of the factory to the other. The steel claws of the machine encircled chicken legs so that their headless torsos and useless wings hung like clothes flapping in the wind on a clothes line. However, the conveyor belt was in constant motion, requiring constant response. The workers stood silently, side by side, reaching with robot-like motions to fulfill specific functions.

One woman repeatedly thrust her lime-colored hands into each chicken cavity, extracting the liver and gizzard. She would do this non-stop for two hours until she reached her ten-minute coffee break or half-hour lunch. I wondered how she could become immune to the sound, smell, and repetitiveness of his job. I now understood the high job-turnover rate. Since camera documentation was not permitted, I used my sketch book to quickly capture the essence of this surreal experience, a trilogy of people, chickens, and machines (Fig. 5).

Before we left Gainesville, Elaine and I had to see the towns monument honoring their proud status as "chicken capital of the world." However, when we arrived at the small park in the middle of town, I was disappointed it was only a bronze, life-size chicken standing on a tall, rectangular pedestal. A tribute to the workers was missing. I would have utilized the worker's lime-green gloved hands to form the chicken's supportive base. I felt dismayed that few people ever realized the robot-like work that had to be completed to prepare the chicken, so casually purchased at the supermarket.

ROSEDALE, ALABAMA
The following day we drove to our next destination, Rosedale, Alabama, a suburb of Birmingham and Freedom from Hunger's only urban project site. As we neared Rosedale, we passed through the neighboring city of Homewood, an affluent white suburban community that had tall office buildings, new shopping centers, and elegant homes. It was a startling contrast with Rosedale, an old African-American community, which was almost completely residential and had old wood-framed houses set along tree lined streets.

The CHAN facilitators, Lee Ann Mortenson and Mari Satterly, met us in front of Rosedale's Lee Community Center. Both women were former Peace Corps volunteers who had been

6. "We Are Troubled on Every Side"

stationed in Africa. In addition to coordinating the Rosedale CHAN program, they were currently enrolled at the University of Alabama's school of public health. Their studies were sponsored by President Clinton's Americorps program, which paid their college tuition in exchange for their community service.

When we entered the center, an emergency food-distribution program was in progress. In an indoor gymnasium tables were set up where families or individuals with low incomes could register and thengo to a nearby room and receive paper bags filled with food prepared by the volunteers.

Lee Ann and Mari introduced us to the food-distribution staff, consisting of eight CHAs, mostly older and retired people, both black and white. I enjoyed seeing the warm embrace of Addy Clay, one of the volunteers who was black, and Lee Ann who was white. I knew I wouldn't have seen this public expression of friendship and cooperation during my first journey to the South.

The CHAs had held their second training session the evening before, and as they prepared the food donations, they told us about the meeting. It had been attended by more than 25 people from Rosedale and Homewood. The main speaker was a staff member of Homewood's St. Vincent's Hospital who gave a presentation about free hospital transportation for cancer patients and the elderly. However, some of the CHAs felt the need for preventative health care and suggested the idea of a mobile trailer that could come to communities such as Rosedale and check blood pressure to prevent the acceleration of treatable diseases. The hospital speaker thought it might be arranged.

"Many people are without cars; therefore there is an urgent need for public transportation as well as more school buses," said Gertrude Williams, one of the CHAs.

She then explained, there were only four elementary schools between Rosedale and Homewood, and because in most families both parents worked, bringing kids to and from school was a problem.

"Parents are so busy trying to make ends meet they have lost the sense of community. If only more people could get together," said Gertrude, stressing that younger people also needed to get involved.

The CHAs seemed to agree Rosedale was the community "most in need" in the Birmingham area, as unemployment was high and crime rampant. The state tax funding was split between Rosedale and Homewood. The CHAs believed the residents of Rosedale were discriminated against by a predominantly white City Council staffed by realtors, who weren't concerned about Rosedale's problems and never gave the city its fair share of tax funding.

The mayor and city council members lived in Homewood. and wanted to expand into Rosedale and buy up more property for commercial enterprises. Through utilizing favorable commercial zoning laws, they were gradually "chipping away at Rosedale." But there was a growing resident resistance.

One of the white CHAs who lived in Homewood, Weda Fritchie, told us she had started up a newsletter several years ago to help keep people informed about the issues behind the scenes. After she published the voting records of Homewood's mayor and City Council, exposing their plans, seven of the eleven council members–and the mayor as well–were replaced in the next election.

"I don't mind calling people racist," Weda staunchly said. Weda wanted her grandchildren to attend an inter-racial school and not be isolated in an all-white community.

CYNTHIA GREATHOUSE   ROSEDALE, AL.

7. "Don't Ask Me"

Although it was apparent that racism and discrimination still thrived in this community, as I talked with the CHAs it was encouraging to meet white people who considered the positive social aspects of integration.

Steffen Waendelin told us how glad he was that many of the CHAs, white and black, were talking together for the first time. They were building awareness and sharing information and together could accomplish what one person alone could not. "It's customary to say, 'We're fixin' to make changes about this or that,' but now we really can," he said.

Lee Ann and Mari then took us to the room where the CHAN meeting had taken place the night before. A senior citizen meeting was just ending and we were introduced to several participating CHA members, including Elmira Shepard and her daughter, Christine McKnight. It was the Bible under Mrs. Shepard's arm, her straightforward facial expression, and the twinkle in her eye—apparent even behind her eyeglasses—that caught my interest. I soon realized she reminded me of my mother. She looked as if she had weathered many seasons of local history as a participant rather than a bystander. She also looked like someone that could be depended on. I was very glad when she agreed to let me sketch her and her tall, thin daughter. As I sketched I incorporated a seemingly appropriate quotation that was on the wall behind them: "We are troubled on every side, yet not distressed" (Fig. 6).

When I finished sketching it was noon time, and Lee Ann and Mari reminded us that they had early afternoon classes and if we wanted to tour Rosedale we should begin. As Elaine drove our red, rented car and Lee Ann directed, we passed many streets lined with small, white-painted homes. Clustered closely together, most houses had sagging front porches and looked in need of repair. However, front lawns often had shrubs and flowers that reflected a sense of pride. According to Lee Ann, most people now rented their homes from absentee landlords, but had resided there for several generations and hoped to continue.

As we drove around, Lee Ann and Mari were happy to see Cynthia Greathouse, who had been one of the most vocal CHAs at the organization meeting the night before. She was planting flowers in the front of her house, so we stopped to visit. Cynthia invited us to sit down in her yard and welcomed us with a warm smile that contrasted with her T-shirt that said in bold letters, "Don't Ask Me." When I did ask, about the shirt, she told us, "I always tell people exactly what I think and sometimes it can offend them" (Fig. 7).

Cynthia was concerned about the recent CHA meeting and she seemed glad to discuss the proceedings with Lee Ann and Mari. She was frustrated that some CHAs doubted there could be change in this old African American community that had high unemployment and much alcohol and drug abuse. Cynthia firmly believed there could be.

"I teach my children there is no such word as 'no'. It doesn't exist," said Cynthia. "I want a beautiful community for my children. You can learn from the past, but let's go forward."

Cynthia told us she was responsible for six children, three of her own and three who were brought to her early each morning by a white attorney and his wife. She then drove them to and from school, and all six children played together.

Elaine and I enjoyed Cynthia's vibrant personality and, as we left, Elaine told me, "Just sitting next to Cynthia makes a person feel good. She's a beautiful person, inside and out."

MEMPHIS, TENNESSEE

Originally we had planned to go from Alabama to Mississippi, but we decided to make a small detour to visit The National Civil Rights Museum in Memphis, Tennessee. Elaine had never been to Memphis and I was anxious to compare the city with my memories of 1951.

That evening, as we arrived in Memphis, it was obvious many changes had taken place. There were many signs advertising tourist attractions such as Elvis Presley's Graceland mansion and the Civil Rights Museum. The Salvation Army where I had stayed many years ago had been replaced by a medley of modern chain hotels. But most noticeable was Beale Street. Once a place where only blacks went, it was now a major tourist district where dazzling neon signs advertising jazz and blues clubs competed for the mostly white crowd. Our interest soon waned and we decided to rest up for a morning visit to the National Civil Rights Museum.

The museum was located in the Lorraine Motel, where Martin Luther King had been shot. The exhibits, often life-size reconstructions of recent historical events, offered an unforgettable perspective of recent history.

One exhibit consisted of a lunch counter at a Woolworth's store where six people, black and white, men and women, sat on stools waiting to be served. Two white men stood nearby with hands on hips and belligerent facial expressions.

In a second exhibit, onlookers stood on one side of a store window and, through film projection of the actual event, young people were shown running toward us. The exhibit caption explained that it was January, 1963, Birmingham, Alabama.

Police Use Water, Dogs on Marchers
More than 3,000 protesters filled the jails but the marches continued as hundreds of children stayed out of school to participate. Bill Conner instructed firemen to arm the K-9 Corps to clear away protesters, providing the Civil Rights movement with some of its most shocking images of clothes and flesh slashed by snarling German shepherds, and children blasted by high-powered water hoses.

In a third room, we actually stepped into a real Montgomery, Alabama bus and saw life-size white plaster sculptures of a bus driver anxiously turning his head to look at Mrs. Rosa Parks, who sat passively in the fourth row. Above, where advertisements are usually displayed, the sequence of historical events was recorded in detail, and began:

5:30 p.m. on December 1, 1995. It was after a long day's work that Mrs. Parks had boarded the bus and sat down. When the bus filled, she ignored the driver's repeated request to give up her seat to a white man, and move to the back, to the "colored" section. Rosa Parks was arrested.

Rosa Parks' simple act of courageous protest was one of the many sparks that ignited the Civil Rights struggle in which over the next decade many people, including Martin Luther King and

Andrew Young, would fight to bring about federal laws giving people of all races the constitutional right of access to all public facilities. Now, forty years later, I was learning how some of these laws were interpreted. Unfortunately, law and reality were far from synonymous.

MISSISSIPPI

Our destination in Mississippi was Batesville, a small town off Highway 66 just south of Tennessee. This region had been identified as one of the most impoverished areas in the United States and health problems were experienced by large numbers of the population, especially women, children, and the elderly. While welfare programs and health and education agencies did exist, Elaine explained, their outreach capacity was inadequate. Not only were they frequently underfunded, there was also a lack of coordination among them. They were often located at the edge of town, inaccessible to many poor people who did not have cars. There was no public transportation.

It was mid-afternoon, the weather hot and humid, when we arrived at the Batesville Health Center, located many miles from the center of town. Mary Hoskins, who was not only the Batesvillle CHAN facilitator but also an employee of the Mississippi State Department of Health (MSDH), an organization with which Freedom From Hunger partnered to implement the CHAN program, warmly greeted us in her office cubicle. She was the first African American CHAN facilitator we had met. She told us that being a CHAN faciliator made her work at the MSDH much more effective as she had become more in touch with the community.

When I asked her about her personal life she told us that her family had lived in this region for many generations. Her father died when she was young, and her mother raised seven children alone, but six had worked their way through college and now had professional jobs. Mary's husband was a builder, she told us, and with the help of their three sons they had just completed the construction of their own home. Mary was glad that her sons had helped with the house, because it kept them out of trouble in the summer when there wasn't much for them to do.

Mary said there were very few job opportunities. If a student were lucky he/she could get a part-time job at a fast food restaurant during the summer. Thinking back to the summer I had worked in the plantation, I asked who chopped and weeded the cotton. Mary replied that most of the field work had been mechanized, but still only blacks chopped the cotton.

With Mary as our guide, over the next few days we would travel around Batesville and other towns within Panola, Humphrey, and Quitman Counties to meet CHAs of diverse skills and backgrounds. We would meet the people involved in the program and see the challenges and difficulties they faced.

Charles Blakley

Our first CHA visit began in the small town of Sardis, where we went to the office of Charles Blakley, an attendance officer and a counselor of the Panola County Youth Court. Charles, who welcomed us with a warm smile and sturdy handshake, told us he was responsible for all of the schools in Panola County. It was a job that kept him very busy, and as we talked, he had to stop many times to answer the phone or help those that came in for advice. I got the feeling Charles was the main local community resource

BATESVILLE, MISSISSIPPI

8. CHA Meeting, Batesville City Hall

person, as he seemed to know everything, from what government programs were available to how people could repair their homes.

Charles looked disheartened as he told us that the schools were deteriorating due to a lack of state and local funding. When the public schools became desegregated, many of the upper-class white students were put into private schools. Thus, the politicians and the wealthy families who had previously favored a tax base to support public education were now unconcerned. There was a shortage of teachers, many programs had been eliminated, and drug abuse and violence were on the rise.

Charles told us he was very concerned about three youth gangs and their frequent fights which occurred on school property. One gang was white, another black, while the third was integrated. Summer vacation was a month away, and he thought the fighting would increase when school let out, since there wasn't much to do. He was trying to bring CHAs together to plan summer activities. But to keep the gymnasium open or to initiate special activities, would take funding—something they didn't have.

When I asked if there were any public facilities for the kids to use, he told me there was one large public swimming pool, but it was reserved for whites. "That's the way it has always been," said Mary. I was appalled to hear this, but realized it was one thing to have civil rights laws "on the books" and another to enforce them, especially when people didn't demand change.

Off the Main Road

After leaving Charles' office we traveled 12 miles to the town of Como, where we hoped to meet with another CHA, Beverly Findley. Como, like Sardis, was a very small town with one main street lined with a few stores. Although some of the stores were boarded up, I was beginning to realize, Main Street offered only a small indication of Mississippi poverty.

When we arrived at the new apartment complex where Beverly lived, no one was home. But as we got in the car to leave, I noticed behind her apartments an unpaved road that led to a house that looked like it had been made from odd scraps of wood. We decided to investigate.

As we got closer I was shocked to realize this was someone's home. It was no bigger than a small room, with some attached sheds. It had cement blocks for a foundation, holes in the roof, and broken windows that would give little protection from the elements (Fig. 8).

A child was playing outside, but as I walked over to see if I could take some photographs, she ran inside and soon re-emerged with her mother and some of her brothers and sisters. The mother, an African American woman who seemed to be in her late '40s, looked somewhat surprised to see me. And although her eyes hardly seemed to focus, she said hello to Mary, whom she recognized from the health center.

The woman had recently come to see Mary to find out if she knew of any programs to help fix her home. However, when Mary asked if she had followed through on the housing referrals, the woman responded "no."

As we left, Mary was visibly disturbed. "Some folks have no initiative and won't let you help them," she said. "They are alcohol dependent and do not even try to help themselves!" This family had "slipped through the cracks" and seemed unreachable by social services, but I wondered about the future of the children. Was it too late to reach them?

The Batesville CHA Meeting

That evening we went to the Batesville City Hall, a small building on Main Street with a prominent American flag, where a CHA meeting was being held. The theme of the meeting was violence prevention, but only a small number of people, black and white, were in attendance (Fig. 9).

After everyone placed their chairs around in a circle, Mary introduced Elaine and me to the group. Dr. Dennis Frate, a professor of anthropology at Oxford's University of Mississippi, began the meeting by reading the results of a CHA-initiated survey, concerning school violence. The survey, in which students, teachers, and parents had participated, confirmed that violence was disrupting the learning process. Almost 50 percent of the students and 25 percent of the teachers reported knowing someone who carried a weapon to school during the past month. And 20 percent of the students reported experiencing a daily fear for their safety.

As the CHAs discussed the results, they all seemed in agreement that the best immediate solution was the creation of stricter behavioral policies and programs to be enforced by the schools, parents, and students. Because they also felt that the violence was partially a result of not having any organized after school programs, they decided another immediate goal was to expand recreational programs. The CHAs had many ideas for programs, including renting the school gymnasium for the summer, developing sports teams, and having craft activities. However, one of the most interesting suggestions was given by the CHA, Rosalyn Brunt, who suggested providing a mobile library service.

Rosalyn told the group she had initiated a similar project last year, which used volunteers to deliver books to people in rural homes who were without transportation. The program had been quite a success. "People were very grateful," said Rosalyn, "and they always returned the books in good condition." Since budget cuts had eliminated all funding for such programs, more would have to be raised, and it was suggested that funds could be solicited from local businesses and corporations. Elaine said she would try to help, as grant writing was her specialty.

When Elaine asked the CHAs what kids normally did in the summer, they replied "nothing." In the past finding activities for kids to do hadn't been a problem, as most families lived in the country and the kids did chores, gardened, or went to the creek to swim. However, now that most families lived closer to town, as parents were employed in local manufacturing industries, there was little for school-age children to do. It surprised me that no one mentioned integrating the public pool. I wondered if they "lacked initiative" or if they were afraid of losing their jobs.

Three Special CHAs

The next day was our last in this area, as the following day we would drive to Jackson Mississippi, where I would take the plane back to Oregon. While so far I had been very encouraged by the people we had met, this last day would be special. We visited three CHAs whose diverse perspectives broadened our view of Mississippi life and the importance of the CHAN program. Each was committed to addressing specific problems and used their skills and experience to help others and to make positive changes in their community.

Beverly Findley—First, we returned to Beverly Findley's home. She welcomed us into her small but cheerful apartment in which the poster *I Have a Dream*, featuring Martin Luther King, Jr., was prominently displayed.

Findley was a slim gregarious woman in her '40s, but seemed younger despite having a leg brace and walking with a noticeable limp. As we sat on her couch, she told us that in 1986 she had suffered a stroke which had paralyzed most of her body. At first her face was paralyzed and her speech impaired, but with time she had healed. Only the use of her left hand and leg was still limited. Walking remained a problem (Fig. 10). "It took two years and much prayer and support from my mother and friends before I could fight off depression, regain self-confidence, and gain a new sense of purpose," said Findley.

Prior to the stroke, she had worked as a meat cutter in a grocery store on main street, but her days were now filled with other activities. She had strong Christian religious convictions and felt that since she had recovered, she should use her life to help others. Each day, unless she was offered a ride or could borrow a car, she walked long distances to fulfill an itinerary of scheduled visits to the elderly and sick. Some needed her advice and others were simply lonely and wanted her company. It was work she loved, and her face lit up as she told us how she had just helped to celebrate a woman's 107th birthday.

Mary called Findley a "natural healer," and I sensed that her cheerful disposition and knowledge of health-care providers (due to her CHA training) was a ray of sunshine for many people. She was also an invaluable role model as she looked past her own disability and suffering to help others.

Lillie Davis—It was recess time at Marks Elementary School, where we went to find Lillie Davis, a retired teacher and CHA member who was now a substitute teacher. As Elaine and Mary went into the school, I lingered in the schoolyard, transfixed by the children, especially the girls who were jumping rope. They seemed like a field of beautiful flowers in their brightly patterned dresses and braided hair fastened with ribbons and beads. They were second and third graders, so young and free and unaware of what lay ahead of them (Fig. 11).

When I entered the school, Elaine introduced me to Lillie Davis. Davis, who appeared to be in her 60s, told me she had retired a few years ago but came back occasionally to substitute. She said she still enjoyed the work, and as I watched her interact with her students, I got the impression she was an enthusiastic but strict teacher who loved her students and wanted them to rise up from their poverty.

Davis told us that when she wasn't working she enjoyed traveling, and had just returned from Australia, where she was the only black person on the tour—she didn't mind. Davis also spent much of her time now working as a CHA, as she thought it was a good way to teach people how to find solutions to their problems. She told us she had divided her CHA group into three sub-groups. One to address problems related to senior citizens, another for education, and the third to find solutions for community recreation.

When Elaine told Davis of her position as a fund raiser and grant writer, Davis told us she had a dream. It was to construct a multipurpose building in this community that could be used for the youth as well as the aged. "With a building we

I HAVE A DREAM

BEVERLY FINDLEY

9. Beverly Findley in Her Home

could do wonders," Davis sighed. I could visualize Davis taking charge and mobilizing people to get things done. She was a very special woman, and it took people like her, who were willing to give back to the community, to make positive changes happen.

M.C. Burke—On the wall outside of M.C. Burke's office in the town of Marks (twenty miles from Batesville) was a wood plaque dated March 21, 1981. The bronze inscription read: "Black Men of Quitman County: We walked 29 days and the walls of opposition fell down."

When we entered his office, Burke, who was the Director of Big River Housing and Development Corporation as well as a CHA, greeted us with a firm handshake. When I asked about the significance of "Black Men of Quitman County," he explained that the plaque was a celebration of their victory against racism. The White City Fathers of Marks would not grant him or other Black people building permits, so for 29 days they marched around the town until "the walls of opposition fell down."

Burke told us he was a Mississippi University graduate, and that he worked in conjunction with the federal department of Housing and Urban Development (HUD) to assist people who lived in impoverished conditions by repairing or rebuilding their homes. Not only did he do the administrative work and grant writing, but also much of the designing and planning construction (Fig. 12).

When I asked Burke why he came back to this region, \as he had professional alternatives, he responded: "I didn't see many changes here, and young people need role models. I want to make a difference."

As a HUD contractor, Burke worked with poor whites as well as black people, and he had many stories to tell. He remembered a poor, elderly white woman who had come to his office and applied for housing improvement. The women had qualified for the HUD housing program, but when she realized that Burke was the program director and not just the carpenter, she refused to participate. Her racist pride would not allow her to receive help from a black person. Burke was sure that she still lived in the same house, which he described as "rodent infested, with holes in the ceiling, and grass growing through the floor boards"—similar to the house we had seen in Como.

According to Burke this was the status of at least one-fourth of the homes in Mississippi. When we asked Burke if he could tell us of any specific towns we should visit to see more examples of typical Southern poverty, he said, "just drive off the main street and along back roads in *any* town."

Like Davis, Burke was very special, as he gave back to the community in which he had been raised. But I was also impressed with his fighting spirit. Maybe if there were more people like him the swimming pool in Como would be open to people of all colors.

CONCLUSION

As in Thailand, this journey served as a reality bridge between my previous experiences and the present. While there had been some very positive changes, I was very disappointed in the extreme poverty and racism that I found.

When I returned to Oregon, I remembered my painting Play Free that I did in response to the Los Angeles Watts Riots of 1964. In the painting, there is a small child with her arms

LILLY DAVIS

10. Lillie Davis at Marks Elementary School

outstretched, as she symbolically reaches out to claim her right to play free. The girl in the painting reminded me of the children jumping rope at the Mississippi elementary school.

While the racism I experienced 42 years ago still prevails, it is in a more clandestine form. People of color face a reality of poverty, poor health, and inability to obtain a good education. However, working in segregated factory towns, or living in sheds-of-misery hidden behind Main Street, they are often unnoticed by most Americans of First World status.

Freedom from Hunger's programs were working to identify and focus attention on these people. The CHAN facilitators provide the link for people of varied ethnic, economic and educational backgrounds to work together. CHAs such as Beverly Findley, Lillie Davis, and M.C. Burke, through their hard work, revitalize the spirit of hope and the possibility of change, so that in the future children can have not only the opportunity to "play free" but also to become productive and healthy adults.

11. M. C. Burke at His Desk